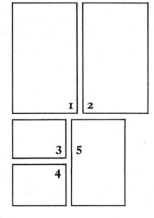

| | |
|---|---|
| **I** | **2** |
| **3** | **5** |
| **4** | |

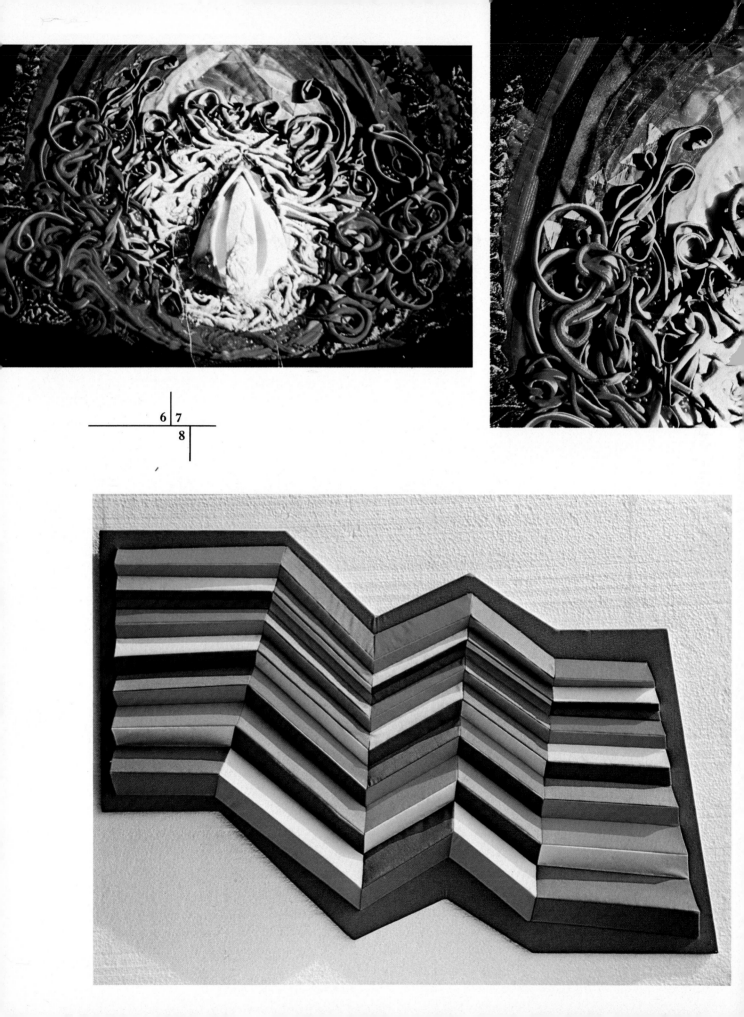

6 | 7
8

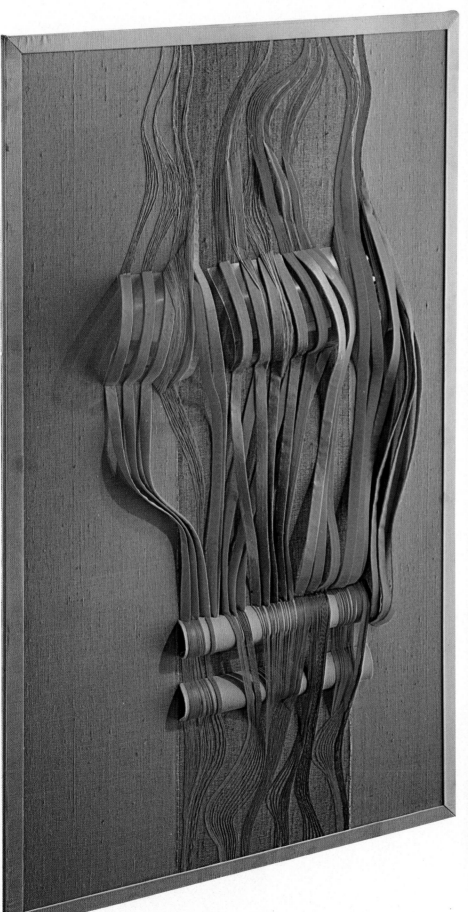

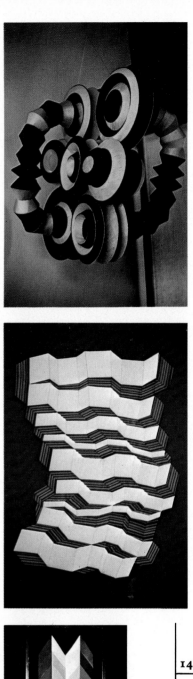

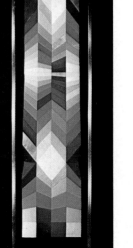

13 | 14
   | 15
   | 16

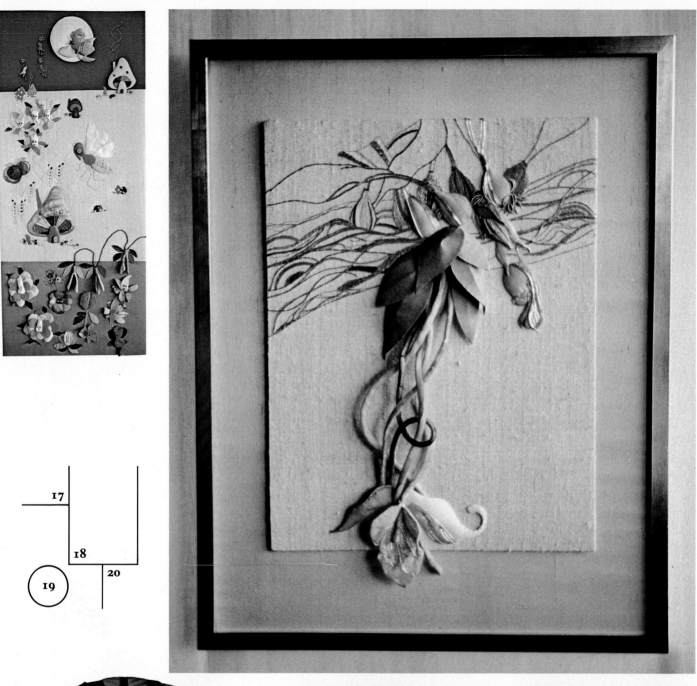

17

18

19

20

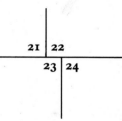

21 | 22
23 | 24

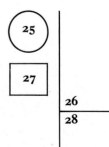

# Three-Dimensional

# Embroidery

HANNAH FREW

VNR VAN NOSTRAND REINHOLD COMPANY
NEW YORK · CINCINNATI · TORONTO · LONDON · MELBOURNE

Van Nostrand Reinhold Company Regional Offices:
New York Cincinnati Chicago Millbrae Dallas

Van Nostrand Reinhold Company International Offices:
London Toronto Melbourne

Library of Congress Catalog Card Number 74–9188
ISBN 0–442–30075–1 (cl.)
ISBN 0–442–30085–9 (pb.)

Designed by David Bethel
Jacket design by Jerzy Karo

This book is set in Monophoto Imprint and
printed in Great Britain by Jolly & Barber Ltd, Rugby

Published by Van Nostrand Reinhold Company Inc.,
450 West 33rd Street., New York, N.Y. 10001,
Van Nostrand Reinhold Company Ltd.,
Molly Millar's Lane, Wokingham, Berkshire, and
Van Nostrand Reinhold Australia Pty. Ltd.,
17 Queen Street, Mitcham, Victoria 3132.

16 15 14 13 12 11 10 9 8 7 6 5 4 3 2 1

Library of Congress Cataloging in Publication Data

Frew, Hannah.
Three-dimensional embroidery

Bibliography: p.
1. Embroidery. I. Title.
TT770. F7          746.4'4          74–9188
ISBN 0–442–30075–1
ISBN 0–442–30085–9 pbk.

# Contents

# Captions to Colour Plates

Colour plate 1. Pipes.
*Drain pipes; gas pipes;*
*Water pipes; oil pipes;*
*Hide them away! Box them in! Hide them in lofts;*
*Cover them with floorboards; Cover them with walls;*
*Don't admit to having pipes!*

*Paint your pipes the same colour as the walls –*
*Nobody will notice them then.*
*Box in your water pipes*
*Under the bath, under the sink,*
*Your streamline kitchen doesn't have room for pipes –*
*Hide your gas pipes under the floor, above the ceiling;*
*Don't admit to having pipes!*

*What's wrong with pipes anyway?*
*Why can't they have a place in the home?*
*Why can't they be painted bright colours?*
*Why can't they match the curtains, match the carpet?*
*Be extravagant with your pipes!*

Christine Simpson

Colour plate 2. Landscape. *Unusual colour effect achieved by inserting selected arrangements of short lengths of coloured wools into polythene tubing, which is then looped against a background of black and brightly coloured towelling. 36 × 42 ins. (91·5 × 107 cm.)* Mary Gribble.

Colour plate 3. Tarmacadam Road Kills Wild Flowers. *The outside of the box is covered with grey gingham, with a band of white P.V.C. along the centre opening to represent the roadway. Inside, the box is filled with flowers of the hedgerow and the small insects and animals dependent on them.* Lorna Benson.

Colour plate 4. Sand Ripples. *Development from drawings of sand, the embroidery being carried out in quilting and laid gold threads.* Christine Simpson.

Colour plate 5. Clear Water in Rivers. *Ribbons are used to give the downward movement of the water, and padded areas represent the turbulence at the base of the waterfall. Conservation theme, directed towards the prevention of water pollution. 19 × 26 ins. (48 × 66 cm.)* Linda Spence.

Colour plate 6. White Heat. *Fabrics are made into rouleaux, then coiled and twisted on the background, creating textural movement.* Kirsty McFarlane.

Colour plate 7. *Detail of* White Heat.

Colour plate 8. Patchwork Panel. *The basic patchwork design is made over cardboard templates, which are left in position when the work is completed. The embroidery is then pushed into a concertina-type formation and held in place on a shaped background, following the outline of the design.* Ann Kennedy.

Colour plate 9. Drawn Thread Sampler. *An interesting surface is created by the use of colour, and pulled and raised thread techniques. Small sections of differently coloured plain weaves are pieced together after each section is altered by withdrawing threads partly or completely, and the remaining threads are treated in a variety of ways.* Hannah Frew.

Colour plate 10. Humpy Bumpy Quilt. *The result of an investigation into the properties of material when cut in circles. The fluting arrangement, caused by the way the fabric is cut, is controlled and held in place by shaped gussets.* Margaret Hinshaw.

Colour plate 11. Gold and Silver. *Various combinations of laid metal threads, involving different methods of couching in order to control the play of light on the surfaces. The centre circle is padded in layers from background level in the centre to approximately ¼ in. (6 mm.) at the outer edge. The large triangular shapes are also made in layers mounted over card, having two small triangles on the top surface, and they in turn support the larger circle which spans the central golden panel.* (Presented by Margaret Oppen to the Embroiderers' Guild of New South Wales, Australia.) Hannah Frew.

Colour plate 12. Golden Disc. *A chequerboard arrangement of colour gradations, pierced by a circle of goldwork which becomes progressively deeper towards the centre.* (Property of Mr and Mrs H. J. White, New York.) Hannah Frew.

Colour plate 13. Karraree Fire. *Observation of flames licking around logs inspired this design, which explores the use of fabrics and threads to create similar movement to that of the flames. 24 × 40 ins. (61 × 101·5 cm.)* Hannah Frew.

Colour plate 14. Mobile. *A free-hanging object created from circular units. This design is a further development from the theme which produced the* Humpy Bumpy Quilt *(colour plate 10).* Margaret Hinshaw.

Colour plate 15. Steps of Illusion. *Three-dimensional impression achieved by perspective drawing and exploiting the use of striped cotton and the light-catching properties of cotton satin.* Lindsay Hoyle.

Colour plate 16. Blue Towers. *Both implied and actual three-dimensional design combine to increase the impression of height and depth. Careful use of colour gradation and the use of perspective add to this effect.* (Photographic Department, Glasgow School of Art.) Margaret Hinshaw.

Colour plate 17. Nursery Panel. *Fanciful flowers and imaginary creatures stand out from a softly padded background composed of three colours, which creates the illusion of landscape. 22 × 50 ins. (56 × 127 cm.)* Marion MacKay.

Colour plate 18. Orchids. *Fine silks and plain and printed chiffons are mounted over carefully modelled foundation shapes. These are then made into rouleaux and combined with laid silks and metal threads to create a three-dimensional expression from a drawing of orchids. 19 × 24 ins. (48 × 61 cm.) approximately.* Lindsay Hoyle.

Colour plate 19. Large Flower. *Hand and machine embroidery on varied textural surfaces ranging from towelling to P.V.C.* Christine Simpson.

Colour plate 20. Bunch of Flowers. *Decorative flower heads created by interesting use of gathering and padding, after being embroidered with sequins, beads, and stitchery.* Christine Simpson.

Colour plate 21. Peppers Hanging. *Design evolved from drawings of green peppers. The cushions are made of silk worked in batik, enmeshed in free, open knitting. The seeds are made of brightly coloured satins over firm padding, and hung on cords. 30 × 58 ins. (76 × 147 cm.)* Marion MacKay.

Colour plate 22. Discotheque. *Almost life-size figures made on plywood backing, and padded out in various depths. The garments are made from different fabrics, embroidered, printed, and plain. The features are embroidered, and hair created from hemp or wool.* Mary Pilpak.

Colour plate 23. Parliament of Animals. *A conservation project led to this design of animals meeting to discuss their future. The animals are padded, moulded, and covered with carefully selected textural fabrics appropriate to each animal, for instance velvet for the elephant and scraps of fur for the monkey.* (Property of Mr T. MacKay, Architect, Glasgow.) Marion MacKay.

Colour plate 24. Apples. *Design based on observational drawings of apples, carried out in satins, silks, chiffons, and fine leather on a felt background.* (Property of Miss H. K. R. Whyte, Eaglesham.) Mary Gribble.

Colour plate 25. Inset Panel for a Communion Table. *Three-dimensional passion-flower made of silks moulded over stiffening to form the petals, which are then embroidered with silks. The flower is mounted over a circle of delicately drawn vine leaves in gold threads and organza, on a background of orange heavy silk.* (Property of Sherbrooke St Gilbert's Church, Glasgow.) Mary Pilpak.

Colour plate 26. Pulpit Fall. *The shadow cross on the turquoise panel is made of patchworked strips in a gradation of dark to mid-toned blues. The simple gold cross is triangular in section with a slender gold embroidered circle outlining the central detail. The three-dimensional effect grows outward from the central solid gold circle, which is couched in arcs, echoing the lines formed by the stepped areas of colour leading up to the outer edge.* (Property of Lesmahagow Parish Church, Lanarkshire.) Hannah Frew.

Colour plate 27. Passion-Flower Pulpit Fall. *Design based on the passion-flower, surmounted by a cross which is given the appearance of a Celtic cross by the circle of the 'crown of thorns' on the passion-flower. Silks, folded and pleated, with stitchery in some areas, form the main part of the flower. The cross is made of silver leathers, purl and laid metal threads over a stiffening of cardboard and balsa wood.* (Property of Colmonell Church, Ayrshire.) Hannah Frew.

Colour plate 28. Detail of Cross Pulpit Fall. *The gold cross has an open-work centre of raised embroidered sections, and scrolling lines of metal threads on a blue silk circle. The legs of the cross are in gold kid mounted over card. In the exact centre of the cross is a square of shisha glass, which reflects the image of the viewer.* (Property of Kirkton Parish Church, Carluke.) Hannah Frew.

# Acknowledgements

Parliament of Animals *(see Colour plate 23.)*
*Modern 'stumpwork' panel, showing individual
treatment of the animals, and disregard of relative sizes.*
Marion MacKay

I would like to thank present and former students of the
Embroidery and Weaving Department of the Glasgow
School of Art for giving me permission to publish
photographs of their work, and Mr Barnes and mem-
bers of the staff of the Glasgow School of Art for their
help and encouragement, especially Miss H. K. R.
Whyte, Ralph Burnett, Francis B. Dunbar, Edward
Odling, Robin C. Rennie, and Mrs. J. A. G. Rowan.

I am particularly grateful to Carol Jones and Ann
and Kate Dunnett, who read the manuscript, and to
Sheila Tickle and Carolyne Murison for typing. I am
also grateful to the Victoria and Albert Museum and
the U.K.A.E.A. Film Library for help with photographs, and to owners of embroideries for permission
to include pieces of work in their possession.

To Tom, John, and my parents for
their constant encouragement and help.

*Hannah Frew*

# 1. Introduction

Embroidery has never really been thought of as a completely two-dimensional craft, as reference to the history of embroidery will reveal, but as artists and designers become increasingly conscious of space, the emphasis in design is moving towards the development of shape and form. The creation of textural forms and raised surfaces involves the embroiderer in a wider range of investigation, and brings into use various methods of working other than the traditionally accepted use of stitchery on fabric. (Figs. 1 – 1 and 2.)

This area is only just beginning to be explored and there are countless possibilities still untried. However, in the excitement of creating new forms and original textures, the fundamental properties of design, craftsmanship and quality must be retained and re-examined constantly in order to maintain the standards that good embroidery demands.

All the work shown in this book has been produced by students or former students of the Glasgow School of Art, which has a strong tradition of embroidery associated with famous names such as Jessie Newbery, Ann MacBeth, Kathleen Mann and, in recent years, Kathleen Whyte. Individual students are encouraged to develop their own personal approach to design, which can be clearly seen in their choice of subject and their methods of presentation. In the earlier stages of the embroidery diploma course at Glasgow, certain set projects are tackled, resulting in a series of solutions which on the surface appear to be similar. (Figs. 1 – 3, 4 and 5). However, even within these strict limitations each individual student usually produces something quite personal, which will lead to more advanced experiments and developments. (Fig. 1 – 6.)

Considerations of space, both open and enclosed, have become major issues in present day living. Areas of open, natural countryside are being encroached upon by the inventions and developments of man. Each development produces a new set of shapes which have to be considered in relation to our ever decreasing natural environment. Proportions are constantly changing, creating different balances between concrete and

Fig. 1 – 1. White Hanging. *Subtle bas-relief design using simple white wool embroidery on a natural coloured background. 34 × 56 ins. (86·5 × 142 cm.).* Jennifer Hex.

Fig. 1-2. *Detail of* White Hanging.

sky, buildings and natural foliage. This balance is of tremendous importance, as all planners should realise. The tendency is to believe that any new development is bound to be bad, but perhaps it is just that our natural instincts revolt against such changes in our surroundings. There is tremendous visual excitement in the unexpected – such as the huge sphere of an experimental nuclear reactor surrounded by natural landscape. (Fig. 1-7.)

The observations in this book are on a more personal level (Figs. 1 – 8 and 9); nevertheless similar emotions are involved in considering the third dimension in relation to textile art. Materials and threads, being pliable and textured, provide the practical means to express those design ideas and thoughts behind the creation

Fig. 1-3. *A yard of hessian used as a design medium. Fraying and knotting methods were used, and the material was then attached to a metal ring at the top, to hang as a cylindrical form.* Carolyne Murison.

Fig. 1–4. *First year student's experiment with fabric to discover design possibilities.* Robert Munn.

Fig. 1–5. *Another experiment with fabric, discovering rhythms from thread loops.* Janet McNair.

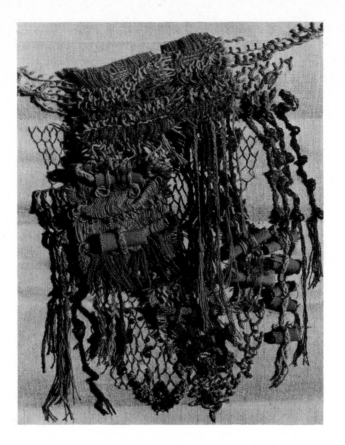

Fig. 1–6. *Experimental panel using materials, stitchery, and cords over an undulating background. 16 × 24 ins. (41 × 61 cm.).* Margaret McFedries.

Fig. 1–7. *View of the Experimental Fast Reactor at Dounreay, seen from the rocks.* (United Kingdom Atomic Energy Authority.)

Figs. 1–8 and 9. *Close-up detail of a shell and a piece of bark, which could be the inspiration for a textural experiment in fabrics.*

Fig. 1–10. *Design of padded shapes and connecting lines, inspired by the quality of the material and the interesting shape possibilities found in scraps of fine leather from a glove manufacturer. 22 × 30 ins. (56 × 76 cm.) approximately.* (Photographic Department, Glasgow School of Art.) Ellen Knap.

Fig. 1–11. *Detail of* Karraree Fire *(see Colour plate 13). Light and shade give definition to different surfaces and shapes. Lines of thread create light curving shapes in contrast to the heavier semi-circular bands.* Hannah Frew.

of three-dimensional surfaces or forms. (Fig. 1–10.)

The simple act of bending a flat rectangle into a cylinder suddenly brings the shape into life, making it 'real'. (Colour plate 1.) This reality of the third dimension stems from the fact that everything one handles has form and shape; even a flat piece of paper will bend, fold, or crumple into a form. We accept the forms around us as normal, and do not become particularly aware of them unless they possess some striking feature which attracts our attention and leads to closer observation. Fostering an awareness of space and studying the relationship between forms will lead to a greater sense of this aspect of design – notice, for

instance, the way light defines different surfaces, and the reaction of these surfaces when the direction of the light changes. Light and shade give definition to form. They tell our eyes what kind of shape they are observing; whether it is a smooth, faceted surface or a rough, undulating area. This may seem a very basic and obvious point, but because we tend to accept forms in space instinctively, it is essential to create conscious awareness of these simple relationships.

The observation of contrasting forms and surfaces and the effect of light directed on to them will be reflected in the embroiderer's choice of fabrics and the way they are used to create textural works from three-dimensional studies. (Colour plate 2.) Individual approaches vary according to the designer's personal interests. Consequently this book contains selected examples, covering as wide a range of textural, three-dimensional work as possible.

The boundaries between the various areas of artistic expression have tended to be disregarded for a number of years, with the result that it is not always possible to describe a work specifically as either one thing or another; for example, a piece of work might be looked at as a three-dimensional painting, or as a sculpture with the addition of colour. Embroidery, too, can be closely associated with many other means of expression – sculpture, painting, jewellery, print, weaving, etc. – but the essential requirement of an embroidery is that it must retain the inherent qualities of threads and their use in relation to textile materials. The embroidery designer should aim to achieve this sympathy with the chosen medium, rather than straining its resources to extremes in order to achieve something 'new'. True originality is achieved by applying a fresh approach to the basic properties of the materials and techniques, and not by imposing gimmicks from outside the craft.

Three-dimensional work, in particular, runs the risk of becoming superficial and forced, unless the stimulus originates in the properties of materials and threads and their ability to drape and mould themselves over forms and shapes.

The third dimension spans a wide range of the use of space, varying in degree from raised textural surfaces on a flat ground, through progressive depths of bas-relief, to objects which are completely in the round. The entire range is so vast that it would be impossible to explore every aspect personally, but an awareness of all the possibilities will produce specific interests which can be developed further.

Closely involved with three-dimensional design are the properties and qualities of light. Its importance in this context cannot be over-emphasised, since it not only highlights the shape of forms, bringing interest and definition to their surface qualities, but it also controls, to a great extent, the balance of a composition. (Fig. 1–11.) The types of shape used in a composition create a clear impression, which is accentuated by the quality of light and shade, either producing sharp, strong definition, or softly rounded surfaces which merge into shadows. The careful selection of tones and colours in the materials used can add to the sculptural appearance of the work.

In many instances the impression of a raised surface can be achieved two-dimensionally by carefully manipulating shape, tone, and colour. This aspect has been explored in many of the visual arts, and the theories developed from experiments and the study of perspective and optical illusion can also be applied to textiles.

Personal observation and imagination will assist the designer in the initial stages of designing for embroidery, but a thorough knowledge and understanding of materials and techniques will enable those ideas to be realised in a completely satisfying manner. The study of traditional embroidery techniques not only widens the scope of design, but may also offer the embroiderer more original ideas for methods of working a three-dimensional design.

It is not always easy to dissociate certain techniques from their normal method of application, but much can be gained from looking afresh at embroidery methods and discovering new ways of producing design ideas in materials. It can be a rewarding exercise, for instance, to work in a completely different scale from the one normally adopted, finding in the process that materials and some techniques adapt in an unexpected way to the change of size and method of working.

There is virtually nothing new in the realm of embroidery; only in the individual designer's approach to the fundamental properties of the craft can originality find its expression.

# 2. Historical Reference

Throughout the history of Western embroidery, indications of the search for three-dimensional expression may be found. Many examples, as far back as *Opus Anglicanum* (12th – 14th centuries) and even earlier, show the embroiderer's desire to explore the possibilities of depth, either by the subtle use of threads and stitchery to imply volume, or in the actual creation of form. The figures portrayed in many fine pieces of ecclesiastical embroidery worked within the period from the 12th century until the end of the 14th century were modelled by the careful direction of lines of stitchery to produce the rounded appearance of features and drapery. (Fig. 2–1.) Biblical characters were very sensitively drawn, their personalities being accentuated by clever use of detail, and facial modelling which was achieved by using stitchery in spirals. Towards the end of this great period in the history of embroidery, techniques were developed to include actual

Fig. 2–1. *Detail from the* Syon Cope. *Coloured silks and silver gilt thread in split stitch and underside couching on linen. English 1300–20.* (Victoria and Albert Museum, London.)

Fig. 2–2. *Detail of coverlet of quilted linen. English, 1703.* (Victoria and Albert Museum, London.)

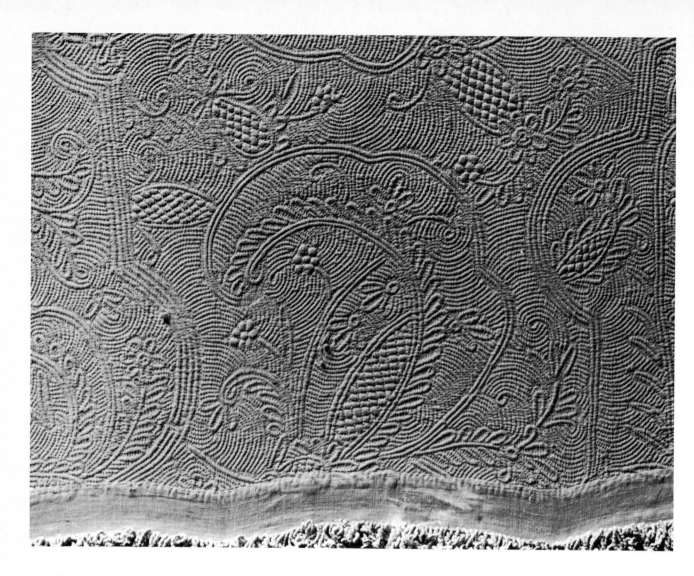

Fig. 2–3. *Part of coverlet. Quilted cotton. English, early eighteenth century.* (Victoria and Albert Museum, London.)

padding and raised work methods in the working of figures on some of the famous English copes.

There is evidence to prove that the technique of quilting existed many hundreds of years before this great era of church embroidery. It is difficult to establish definite information about examples because of the effect of time on textiles, but from carvings and pieces of floor covering discovered during excavations in different parts of the world it is clear that this technique was used fairly extensively both for garments and for domestic use.

There are many gaps in the history of quilting, but it is safe to assume that it has been used almost continuously throughout the centuries in both a practical and a decorative way. Bed coverings have been produced by this method until the present day (Figs. 2–2 and 3), although the word 'quilt' has now lost its original meaning and is used to describe various types of bed-

covering other than the traditional quilted cover. The fact that wadding or padding is inserted to produce the raised surface creates the additional effects of warmth and strength, giving the technique of quilting unique qualities. These qualities have been used to advantage in various ways through the years, depending on the particular needs of the time. For instance, quilted garments were worn under armour to provide protection from the heavy metal. Indeed, before metal armour was in use, protective clothing made of quilted linen was worn to safeguard the body in battle. As the need for that type of garment disappeared, quilting became more decorative, still providing warmth and comfort, but now incorporating colour and pattern to enliven and beautify clothing. (Figs. 2–4 and 5.)

The fashion for elaborately quilted garments in the 17th and 18th centuries, which gave the technique broader scope and lighter, more decorative application,

Fig. 2–4. *Dress embroidery sample. Areas of threads withdrawn in one direction from background material padded with Italian quilting cotton, and held in place by lines of zig-zag machine embroidery.* Ellen Knap.

led to the combination of Italian quilting and fine drawn fabric fillings.

The main evidence of attempts to produce embroidery in the round is to be found in stumpwork, which was produced in the period between about 1650 and 1680. This work had its roots in the methods employed by Elizabethan embroiderers in working raised metal thread embroidery and detached buttonhole stitched areas. (Figs. 2–6 and 7.) The pictorial decoration, involving various motifs, required very fine, painstaking methods. The childlike simplicity of these pictures is attributed to the work being done mainly by young girls who had an extremely high degree of practical ability as craftswomen.

These embroideries were generally worked on a background of white or ivory-coloured satin. They may have been purchased with the main design already printed on the background, but it is evident that the

Fig. 2–5. *Dress embroidery sample. The techniques of Italian quilting and machine embroidery are combined using single and treble needle on a foundation of colourful striped silk.* Ellen Knap.

individual motifs were taken from pattern books of that time. The subject matter was very often taken from stories from the Old Testament, showing figures such as David and Bathsheba in a fantastic landscape, generally including a castle and possibly a fountain playing in the foreground, all the intervening spaces being filled with animals, flowers, butterflies, and birds, with clouds, sun, and moon completing the picture. The over-all impression of these pictures was always the same, for the figures, whether biblical characters or royal personages, were always portrayed in 17th century costume. The settings, too, were always similar, and no attention was paid to the relative proportions of foreground and background motifs. (Fig. 2–8.) Each figure or animal was shown standing on its own individual hillock, and very often the flowers or animals were worked in different techniques, so that one flower might be produced in fine canvas work and then applied to the background; another done in laid silks; and yet another modelled from the background by being worked in detached buttonhole stitch. Faces were often made from carved wood or ivory, while hands, if not made in this method, were ingeniously carried out in other ways, such as wire closely wound with silk. The addition of small pearls and precious stones often helped to enrich the effect, while each costume was carefully represented with minute attention being paid to detail. This portrayal of fashionable, richly clad figures demonstrates the lively enthusiasm the young embroiderers had for their subject. No doubt young girls enjoyed the freedom of working on these decorative panels, allowing their imagination to run freely, after the restrictions of the formal, painstakingly embroidered samplers they had to execute in order to learn their craft.

Although there is such strong similarity in all the surviving pieces of stumpwork, each young artist has used her imagination and ingenuity in dealing with details of garments and features. The finished panels were mounted in a variety of ways, as book covers, mirror frames, pictures (Fig. 2–9) or caskets (Fig. 2–10). The insides of the caskets were often fitted with a number of small drawers and compartments, each with its embroidered front covering, surmounted by a pastoral scene or possibly a garden worked completely three-dimensionally. During this period of stumpwork, beads were also being used in the execution of various articles involving raised work. They were more durable than silks or metal threads, and their bright colours were often used to great effect.

Beadwork continued in popularity long after stumpwork had gone out of fashion, disappearing from the embroidery scene towards the end of the 17th century. Beads were often strung on to fine wire and used three-dimensionally to create flowers, butterflies, and many of the other motifs so popular in Elizabethan and Stuart embroidery. These were again used in creating

Fig. 2–6. *Purse. Canvas embroidered with coloured silks and silver thread in detached buttonhole stitch, with seed pearls, metal loops, and coils. Lined with brocaded silk. English, late sixteenth or early seventeenth century.* (Victoria and Albert Museum, London.)

elaborate caskets, trays, pictures and so on, just as in stumpwork. As the use of beads developed and the manufacture of glass beads was improved, beadwork became more refined and greater detail was achieved in producing fine jewel cases, purses, etc., and also decoration for waistcoats, neckbands and baby clothes. Beadwork reverted to being coarse and rather gaudy in the late 19th century, although some fine examples are to be found among Victorian work.

The application of embroidery techniques to garments makes interesting study, as each technique can be associated with particular periods in the history of

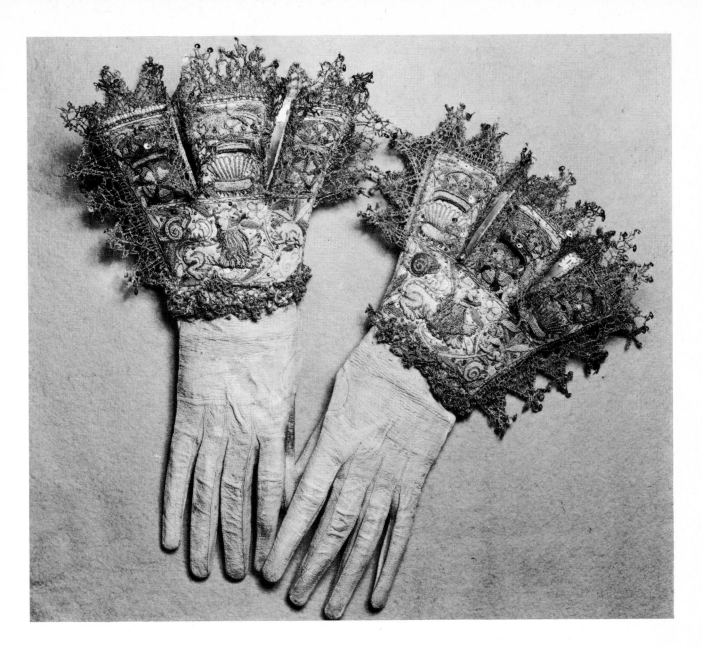

Fig. 2–7. *Pair of gloves. Leather trimmed with satin and embroidered with silk, silver-gilt and silver thread, and seed pearls. Trimmed with gold and silver bobbin lace. English, early seventeenth century.* (Victoria and Albert Museum, London.)

costume as well as reflecting certain aspects of the social background of the particular time.

With the coming of the Industrial Revolution and the manufacturing of fine ribbons and braids, there emerged examples of dress embroidery which used ribbons in such a way as to create a new textural appearance and scale on garments. In some examples the narrow ribbons were worked through the materials just as threads would be, while in others the ribbons were applied to the surface, but generally the three-dimensional quality of the ribbons was shown to advantage by looping or twisting them.

The illusion of depth in design was cleverly used in many of the traditional patchwork designs carried out in the 18th and 19th centuries. The technique of patchwork was very often combined with quilting in the creation of beautiful coverings, but when it was used in its own right, the design possibilities were many and varied. This technique enabled the embroiderer to create rich, colourful patterns through the choice of brightly coloured scraps of material, either plain or printed. The essentially geometric shapes used in the construction of patchwork design, and the experimental placing of tones and colours, resulted in many

Fig. 2–8. *Detail of stumpwork picture (see Fig. 2–9), showing the many different techniques used to portray each section of the design.*

Fig. 2–9. *Stumpwork picture. Embroidered picture with seventeenth-century styled figures and many characteristic motifs, including birds, animals, flowers, castle, and pond.* (Property of Glasgow School of Art.)

interesting designs giving the illusion of three dimensions. These designs appear in many forms through the years and in many different places, proving their popularity and adaptability.

Another embroidery technique which made use of implied three-dimensional design was Berlin wool work, which was extremely popular in the 19th century and was practised in Britain to the exclusion of almost every other type of embroidery. This work consisted of various coloured woollen threads embroidered in cross stitch, tent stitch, and other canvas work stitches into a canvas background. The main effect aimed at was the production of a realistic portrayal of the subject matter, which ranged from bunches of flowers, animals or birds to famous personages. Graded tones of colour were carefully selected in order to create the modelling on the subject. In some pieces of work, tufted or pile stitches were used, and always the surface of the

Fig. 2–10. *Stumpwork casket. Embroidered casket with miniature garden inside the lid. English, third quarter of seventeenth century.* *9 × 11 × 10 ins. (23 × 28 × 25.5 cm.).* (Victoria and Albert Museum, London.)

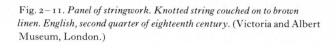

Fig. 2–11. *Panel of stringwork. Knotted string couched on to brown linen. English, second quarter of eighteenth century.* (Victoria and Albert Museum, London.)

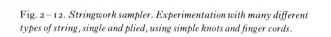

Fig. 2–12. *Stringwork sampler. Experimentation with many different types of string, single and plied, using simple knots and finger cords.*

Fig. 2–13. String Harvest. *Investigating the qualities of string as a design medium: untwisting, knotting and couching. 27 ins (68·5 cm.) square.* Joan Michael.

embroidery was actually modelled by careful clipping and trimming of the tufts of wool.

In patchwork, the designs were produced by arranging flat, mainly straight-edged shapes of different tones, creating an impression of perspective, whereas Berlin wool work endeavoured to create the illusion of smoothly rounded forms by the use of light and shade.

Tracing the origins of embroidery techniques and the application of these techniques throughout history not only leads to interesting discoveries within the craft, but also stimulates the imagination of the designer to investigate the techniques further, in an effort to extend the entire concept of embroidery.

For instance, when studying certain areas of historical embroidery, some interesting examples of stringwork came to my notice. (Fig. 2–11.) This could be the beginning of an investigation into the use of knotted strings, incorporating various types of string and knots. (Figs. 2–12 and 13.) In the same way, examples of embroideries involving straw and ribbons could be the inspiration for experiments in developing techniques of laidwork other than threads. The individual designer will find countless opportunities in the study of historical embroidery for widening the scope and vision of embroidery design.

# 3. Fabrics and Foundations

The basic characteristics and qualities of any fabric come from the type of yarn used in its construction, the spacing of the threads, and the manner in which the threads are woven together. These factors determine the weight, handle, textural appearance and pliability of the material. The choice of fibres and yarns available to textile manufacturers has now become extremely wide and varied, spanning the entire range of natural fibres and the ever-growing selection of man-made yarns.

The result is that the embroiderer is confronted with a vast range of fabrics from which to choose the one most suitable for the purpose. This can be tremendously exciting if one is fortunate enough to have access to the complete range of fabrics, and to be able to handle, study and enjoy them before coming to a decision. Unfortunately, the majority of embroiderers are restricted to the choice of the buyer in their nearest material department, with the possibility of choosing from sample books or small cuttings sent from larger stores which carry comprehensive ranges and stocks. A large number of stores do realise these difficulties and are willing to send a selection of samples on request; however, nothing can replace the excitement of being surrounded by quantities of varied colour and texture which one may handle and choose from.

This initial handling and selecting is of great importance and provides the emotional impetus which carries on throughout a piece of work. (Fig. 3–1.) If the sensitivity of choice and awareness of quality, colour, and texture is lacking in this first stage, nothing can replace it to redeem and vitalise the design. (Colour plate 5.) The textile artist should therefore be intensely aware of the structure and content of all materials, and foster a sensitivity to the feel and appearance of every yarn, fibre, texture, and fabric. (Figs. 3–2 and 3.)

An awareness of colour is apt to control our observation of materials. Colour is a seducer, and tends to dominate our senses, but it must come into line with all the other considerations when a wider study of textiles is developed. (Colour plates 6 and 7.)

Colours react together in woven fabric in a way altogether different from their use in general, because of the nature of the surface and the construction of the weave. An all-over simple but subtle colour effect can be achieved by juxtaposing a number of colours which are closely toned, even though they may come from opposite sides of the colour wheel. Woven fabrics have close associations with the painting technique known as *Pointillisme*, but worked on a smaller and closer scale; this effect depends on the use of spots of colour being placed closely together, and interacting to create subtle colour admixtures. Because of this unique property of woven colour, background fabrics can provide the ingredients for entire colour themes. By carefully analysing the colour content, tonal values, and proportions, and by using the information instinctively, the application of other selected colour on to the background becomes an integral part of the entire work.

The various theories of colour are of interest to all who participate in the visual arts, and it is important to have a certain amount of basic knowledge on which to ground any exploration, but it is only by experimenting and using fabrics that awareness of colour and its excitement can be fully realised.

The surface qualities of materials range through a wide scale of reflecting light effects in countless subtle variations from the dull, matt surface of felt on the one hand to the smooth, shiny gleam of metallic lamé and satin on the other. (Figs. 3–4 and 5.) Within that huge scale there are a great many sub-divisions separating each characteristic group. For instance, woollen fabrics extend through a wide range in themselves, from thick, rough coating materials, through dress-weight fabrics to very fine wool crêpe, just as the silk family has very rough tweed-like silk at one end and fine silk chiffon at the other.

A great deal of this textural contrast is so obvious that it tends to be taken for granted, but real enjoyment of the intricacies of fabric surfaces comes from studying subtle variations within a close area. For instance, there are common factors which link wool and silk crêpe to

Fig. 3 – 1. *Detail of* Red Wall *(see Fig. 8 – 1, p. 86). The effect produced when different types and constructions of materials are frayed, folded, and massed together in a pattern.* Jennifer Hex.

create very similar materials, and yet they have completely different handling and light-catching surfaces. Once again, the best way to acquire this textural knowledge is by simply looking at and handling all kinds of materials, rummaging through any scrap-bag available to discover new textures. Try putting varied fabrics together to see how they react with each other, for instance dull with shiny, and study the heightened effects created by the contrast. Superimpose transparent fabric over different surfaces, such as lurex, satin, or metallic leather, to discover the light and colour changes that can be achieved. It is only in this way that the embroiderer can build up a personal knowledge and sensitivity towards the use of fabrics.

When working three-dimensionally, the selection of materials has to be extended slightly to include the manner or behaviour of a particular fabric in relation to the job to be done. As in all other cases, the factor of

scale and proportion is high on the list of considerations, but in three-dimensional treatment the 'scale' of a fabric has practical as well as aesthetic reasons included in its choice. (Figs. 3–6 and 7.) To state an obvious case, rough hessian would never be used to cover a very small, perfect circle, nor would it be very easy to cover a large padded shape with very fine, soft Jap silk. The scale of the fabric should be included in the appreciation of proportion throughout the complete design.

Certain materials mould and stretch over a foundation shape more readily than others. While similar weight and colour may make the choice between two fabrics fairly even, the fact that one gives an easier, smoother finish over a padded base would determine the final choice. For example, a red silk crêpe would be preferable to cotton poplin of the same colour because of the way the silk yarn is spun and woven.

The problem of easily frayed materials is one that

Fig. 3-2. Falls. *Soft woollen threads used in a variety of techniques including knitting, macramé knotting, and stitchery. Areas of openwork fabric are created as a contrast to the smooth background material. 36 × 50 ins. (91·5 × 127 cm.) approximately.* Mary Wallace.

Fig. 3-3. *Detail of* Falls.

must be considered and tackled in various ways. The fact that a certain material frays readily does not preclude it from being used for covering a raised area, although it is difficult to deal with in particular instances. For example, when dealing with an inside corner, where the material needs to be snipped close to the edge in order to turn it back properly, it is advisable to forestall fraying before cutting the fabric in any way. This can be done either by working a row of machine stitching just inside the cutting line, or by painting a thin line of clear nail varnish along the line to be cut, and allowing it to dry thoroughly before cutting the fabric.

The thickness of the material is another factor to be taken into account. If the area to be covered or padded is of an extremely exact measurement, then the thickness of the covering fabric must be included in the preliminary calculations. Another point to note is that thicker fabrics generally have more 'spring' than finer,

more pliable fabrics. A greater turn-back allowance will solve this problem by enabling the fabric to be secured more easily on the wrong side.

The finished surface appearance of the padded or covered shapes will vary considerably according to the nature of the foundation material. A fabric being used to cover a piece of card or balsa wood will look very different when covering an area of foam rubber. The choice of foundation material is therefore extremely important in that it partly determines the character of an area of work.

Many seemingly useless objects can be turned to good use as basic building materials in three-dimensional work, needing only a little ingenuity to adapt them to the required situation. (Fig. 3-8.) The traditional fabrics used for padding, such as felt and wadding, are always available, but there are also more recent developments such as Polystyrene, plastic tubing, foam rubber,

Fig. 3–4. Rectangles. *Three dimensional design with balsa wood divisions, each area containing arched bars made of sequin waste, silks, and chiffons on a panelled silk background. 22 × 30 ins. ( 56 × 76 cm.).* (Photographic Department, Glasgow School of Art.) Ellen Knap.

Fig. 3–5. *Detail of* Tree. *Ingenious use of materials, beads, and found material such as wood shavings.* Betty Fraser.

etc. Many of these new substances are very light-weight, which is a great advantage. (Figs. 3–9 and 10.) So often, the weight of the built-up areas causes a drag on the background fabric, and this in turn produces an unsatisfactory finish to the embroidery.

Many three-dimensional works require an amazing amount of engineering before-hand, plus very thorough planning, working from the base up to the finished outer surface. Planning involves careful searching for the correct foundation materials, both seen and unseen, on which to build the design. Crispness calls for firm materials such as card or wood, and in order to produce clear, rounded shapes, cardboard tubing or acetate can be used. Polythene tubing or rolled up foam rubber, while basically the same shape, will produce a completely different effect when covered.

Generally speaking, bas-relief designs present fewer problems in dealing with fabrics than those which require the creation of deeper, more rounded shapes. Woven materials are fundamentally two-dimensional surfaces with the ability to drape and cover shapes, and while the structure of the fabric enables it to mould and stretch when used in certain ways – for instance on the cross of the fabric – each material has its limitations. There is a certain point when it becomes necessary to use folding, tucking, darting, or seaming on the fabric to produce a smooth covering for a foundation shape. Basic knowledge of dressmaking can be invaluable.

Basic shapes can be made by a variety of methods, and the substance used will depend on the size and character of the finished area. Very thick foam rubber can be cut and shaped by clipping with scissors; begin

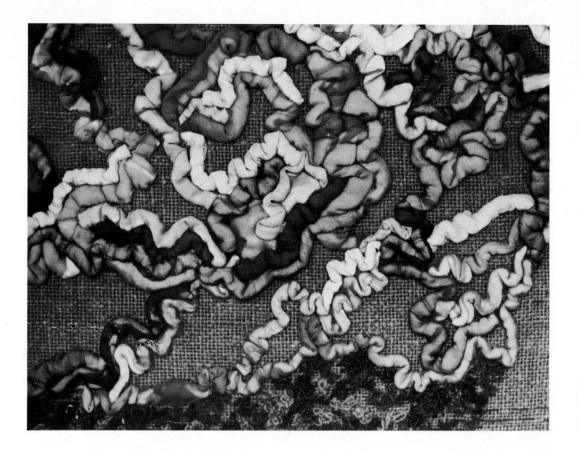

Fig. 3–6. Seashore Composition. *Imaginative treatment of materials to produce large scale textural lines, contrasting with evenweave background material.* Midge Gourlay.

Fig. 3–7. Fir Cones. *Fir cone shapes cut from various leathers and non-fray fabrics, simply attached to the background in layers. 36 × 45 ins. (91.5 × 114.5 cm.) approximately.* Fiona McGeachy.

Fig. 3–8. *Assorted collection of plastic containers for use as foundation material.*

Fig. 3–9. Happy Valley. *Printed fabric, everlasting flowers, small hanks of wool, etc, combined with stitchery on a circular background made of two different materials. 36 ins. (91·5 cm.) in diameter.* Patricia Matheson.

Fig. 3–10. *Detail of* Happy Valley.

by cutting roughly with large scissors, and then smooth it off using smaller scissors and clipping very finely. It is better to over-estimate the size required in foam rubber, because it has a tendency to compress slightly and reduce in bulk when covered with fabric.

Polystyrene requires different handling from any other material mentioned. There are special craft tools available which are heated in order to cut through the surface smoothly and easily – differently shaped wire heads being used for detailed modelling – but it is possible to shape Polystyrene by using a saw or knife.

Large shapes cut out in plywood or hardboard are easier to work on if they are covered or bound with scrap material to begin with, as a foundation for the sewing or padding. This should be done very firmly and secured with strong stitching, dispensing with neatness in favour of stability, so that the foundation will hold fur-

ther layers of padding and materials and remain immovable. Old nylon stockings or tights are useful here, as they stretch very well indeed to mould and cover any awkward shapes. When nylons are cut up into small pieces they also make a very good light-weight padding, and may be used as an alternative to wadding.

More complicated shapes can be produced by bending and shaping wire mesh or chicken wire into the required shape, then covering the rough surface as before with strips of stretchy material, thin foam rubber, *papier mâché*, or wadding to make a good foundation.

A flat sheet of cardboard can become the basis of a raised area, which need not necessarily be angular. The method of producing these shapes is explained in Chapter 5 dealing with geometric forms, and adaptations will create all kinds of raised areas which can be padded and covered.

# 4. Techniques

Traditional embroidery techniques which create designs in relief, such as patchwork and quilting, can be extended and explored when divorced from their accepted application and used to create exciting new possibilities for three-dimensional effects.

## QUILTING

Quilting is the one embroidery technique which instantly suggests form and depth in embroidery. It consists of two layers of material caught together by lines of stitching, generally having a soft layer of padding sandwiched between the two outer layers. This method produces a new thick fabric with a decorative surface created by the indented lines of stitches, and is usually described as English quilting. Variations of this technique include the use of corded lines, when the padding is omitted and quilting cord is pulled between parallel lines of stitching, creating a design of raised lines on a flat background. This is known as Italian quilting. The lesser known Trapunto quilting is done by stitching through two layers of material and inserting padding from the back of the work to accentuate parts of the design.

Quilting has been based very strongly on these traditional methods, and the designs worked were either produced by designers who were famous in their own particular part of the country and had their own distinctive style, or designed by the individual quilter using templates and patterns which were passed from mother to daughter. If we accept this strong background of tradition and convention, but also see the possibilities of stretching the previous limits of the technique as widely as possible, the entire concept is opened up. (Fig. 4–1.)

The beautiful historical quilts can teach us a great deal about the effect of light on padded areas, and while our forbears imposed certain limitations on their work, in that each article was worked as an example of a single technique, thus creating an all-over effect, the modern embroiderer can combine various effects within one design. Naturally, each design idea must be interpreted individually, and demands a certain method of working in order to achieve its effect. Quilting techniques provide exciting possibilities for using gradations of padding throughout a design, ranging from smooth, flat areas to heavily padded sections with variations of Italian quilting or isolated shapes of raised textures.

Apart from the accepted traditional methods of quilting, softly rounded shapes can be achieved in various ways, and a few methods are suggested here:

(a) When a shape is being built up by more than one layer of padding – felt, wadding, or foam rubber – it is better to begin by cutting each successive layer smaller than the previous one; when applying them to the background, however, begin by placing the smallest one in position, then the next one in size on top, and so on, leaving the largest shape for the final layer to ensure a smooth finish for the top surface. (Fig. 4–2.) If the area is being covered by a separate piece of fabric, cover the final layer of padding with the required fabric before applying it carefully to the background; in this way there is no problem with raw edges or ridges made by the hem allowance.

(b) Applied shapes can be padded after being sewn in place on the background by working from the wrong side. Make a slit in the background fabric only, then insert wadding or any other form of padding, pushing it carefully into place from the wrong side, and moulding and controlling it to produce the effect required. Oversew the edges of the slit together carefully and neatly. (Figs. 4–3 and 4.)

This method does not allow the shape to be padded to any great extent; if it were, the background fabric would become distorted by the pull of the wadding.

To prevent the surface becoming lumpy from pushing in the padding on larger shapes, insert before the padding a piece of thin foam rubber cut slightly smaller than the shape; alternatively, line the applied shape either with foam rubber or some other type of stiffening before sewing it in position.

(c) A padded shape can be assembled completely before being placed in position. (Fig. 4–5.) Cut the

Fig. 4−1. Aspidistra. *Triangular based object with triangular shaped 'leaves' curving out from the centre. Each leaf has a quilted surface.* Linda Spence.

Fig. 4−2. *Sample showing layers of felt being applied to form a softly rounded shape. The top layer is covered with silk before being sewn into place.*

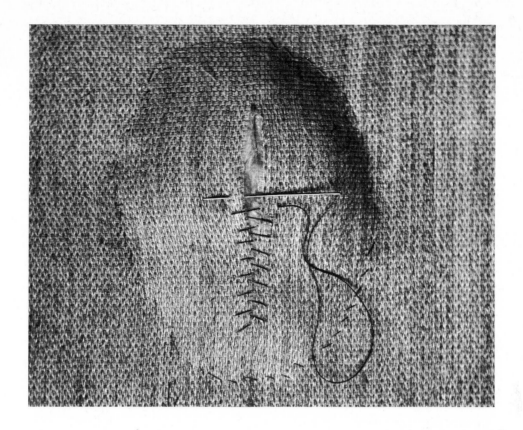

Fig. 4–3. *Wadding has been inserted from the wrong side of the work, and the slit is now drawn together again.*

Fig. 4–4. *Right side of the work, when completed.*

(a)

(b)

(c)

Fig. 4–5. *Sample showing the three stages involved in making a separately padded shape which is then attached to the background. (a) Wadding tacked in position on to the stiffening. (b) The top layer of material being laced across the back of the shape. The edge has been snipped to allow the material to fold smoothly over the curved edge. (c) The shape sewn into position on the background.*

Fig. 4–6. *Detail of* Apples *(see Colour plate 24)*. *Close-up detail of shapes sewn on to the background.* Mary Gribble.

Fig. 4–7. Delta. *White satin padded shapes applied to a background of the same material, with silver metal thread embroidery worked over and between the shapes.* Fiona McGeachy.

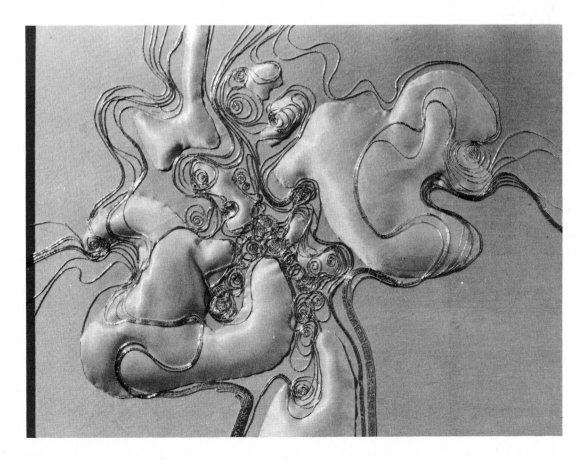

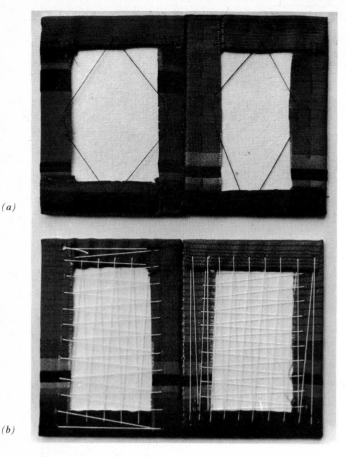

*(a)*

*(b)*

Fig. 4–8. *Patchwork shapes (wrong side). (a) Threads holding material in place over non-woven stiffening. (b) Material laced across with threads over a cardboard shape.*

Fig. 4–9. *Patchwork shapes (right side), showing slight marks left by tacking threads on the silk.*

shape from pelmet stiffening, buckram, or any other firm backing. Then build and pad on top of it before covering the surface with fabric. Turn back the excess fabric to the wrong side of the stiffened base, clipping where necessary to $\frac{1}{8}$ in. (3 mm.) from the edge, to allow for curves. Either tack the fabric in place or lace it in position across the back before sewing the shape to the background. (Figs. 4–6 and 7.)

## PATCHWORK

Patchwork, thought of in its widest sense, consists of joining together pieces of fabric to create a new surface which is decorative in its use of pattern and colour. It is traditionally two-dimensional, and generally practical. The shapes used are usually simple and geometric, enabling the sides of the patches to be sewn together easily. It is only relatively recently that patchwork has been used in a purely decorative way rather than as a piece of functional embroidery which, for practical reasons, was soft and pliable.

Traditionally, when a piece of patchwork is finished

the templates are removed before the article is made up. However, in many of the modern patchwork designs, the stiffening is retained to keep the crispness of the shapes. (Colour plate 8.) By using fine cardboard stiffening, it is possible to create three-dimensional shapes which are remarkably rigid and strong.

Depending on the article being made, either pelmet stiffening or cardboard can be used as the permanent foundation for the shapes. (Fig. 4–8.) In the first case it is possible to tack the covering fabric in place over the stiffening as is normally done in traditional work, but before removing the tacking threads on the completion of the piece of work, catch together the hem allowance at the corners on the wrong side to hold the stiffening in place. When working with card as a foundation, it is often better to hold the fabric in position by lacing across the back of the shape, instead of sewing through the card. Very often tiny marks are left on a plain fabric when the tacking stitches are removed, and lacing the fabric across the back is one method of avoiding this. (Fig. 4–9.)

## DRESSMAKING

While considering the techniques of using fabric to create the third dimension, we can move away from embroidery to think of dressmaking, which also basically consists of joining together pieces of material to create a covering for a three-dimensional form, in this case the human figure. The possibility of incorporating dressmaking methods with patchwork techniques opens many avenues of exploration for making undulating surfaces of exciting colour and texture. (Fig. 4–10.)

Dressmaking is based on the idea that garments are made to cover varied sizes and shapes of people, and methods are adapted to make this possible. (Colour plate 10.) This fundamental thought could well give rise to ideas for creating all kinds of basic shapes which can be padded as firmly as required with many kinds of filling materials, such as wadding, foam rubber, etc.

Fig. 4–10. *Example of curved shapes patchworked together.*

## DRAWN THREAD WORK

Drawn thread work is another embroidery technique firmly rooted in tradition, and with a very definite image. Once again the basic principle of the technique, when examined and explored, offers various starting points for expanding the use of materials in relation to space. (Fig. 4–11.) Withdrawing threads from a piece of material not only alters its appearance but also its reaction to handling in certain ways. (Colour plate 9.)

When it is draped or folded it will have a new appearance. Light can penetrate the structure more easily, and causes new and interesting shadow effects. Different weaves and fabrics give tremendous variation to the use of drawn thread work, and the pattern of traditional stitches worked within this wider scope of the technique provides the necessary contrast to give greater interest and effect.

Fig. 4–11. *Sample of drawn thread work, making use of the three-dimensional looping effect of the withdrawn threads.*

## BEADS

Beads were used in Stuart times to adorn articles and create complicated surfaces, the beads being threaded on to wire, twisted and combined to create flowers, butterflies, etc. Beads in themselves have an extremely interesting history. Different methods of production have brought a great variety in shape, colour, and texture over the ages, but with mass production they are now in danger of becoming very stereotyped and dull.

They are still used extensively in the decoration of certain types of garment, generally adding greatly to the cost of the item because they have to be dealt with by hand.

Each bead has its own characteristic shape and size and is a unit of pattern. The bead units can be used by combining different types to produce many varying areas of three-dimensional textural effects and patterns, not necessarily for dress alone but for other decorative purposes as well. Because they have differing surfaces, light reflections add to the intricate patterns when the beads are placed in layers and rows. (Fig. 4–12.) As they are so completely three-dimensional, they need to be involved in a three-dimensional concept, adding a different approach to the development of textural surfaces. (Figs. 4–13, 14 and 15.)

Fig. 4–12. *Sample of beadwork for application to dress, using clear plastic shapes, crystal drops, clear sequins, and beads.*

Fig. 4–13. *Sample of techniques for dress embroidery, involving among others layers of felt, coloured wooden beads, and punched eyelets laced with handmade cords.*

Fig. 4–14. *Sample of a constructed fabric with possible application to dress. Cardboard and plastic shapes covered with either whipping or button-hole stitch, decorated with beads and sequins, and linked together with embroidered bars.*

Fig. 4–15. *Dress embroidery sampler inspired by drawings of drainpipes piled up in layers. Machine embroidered bands of satin stitch, sequins, pearls, and larger circles cut and punched out in felt.*

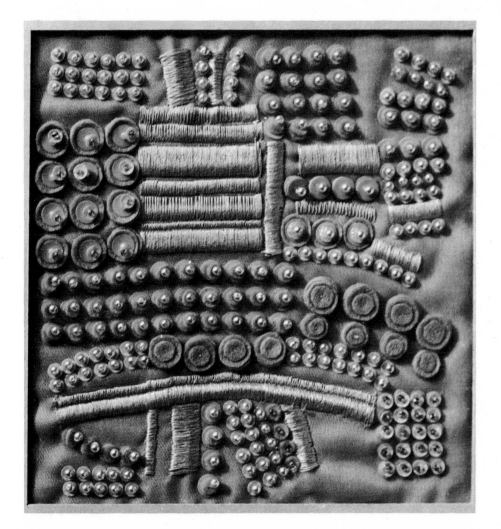

Fig. 4–16. *Balsa wood square to be covered with leather. Leather square shown marked for position, with outer edge skivered.*

## FABRICS

The materials being used to create three-dimensional effects may be chosen from the complete range of fabric qualities, depending on the effect being aimed at and the method chosen to produce the effect. Soft chiffons, wild silks, cotton, hessian, or leather could possibly be the basic fabric and each of these would create its own problems and require an individual approach. Different problems occur depending on the type of shape involved and the quality of the material being used, so it is only possible to give general guidance towards producing a professional effect.

Leather is very strong and springy and therefore requires firmer handling as well as stronger foundation material when being used to build up three-dimensional shapes – in other words, heavier weight card, balsa wood or similar types of foundation material, which will not be too heavy, but which will be strong enough to withstand the pull of the leather.

When covering geometric shapes, cut out the foundation shape in wood or card, making the shape fractionally smaller than required, as the thickness of the leather will bring it up to the correct size. Work out the amount of leather required to cover the shape, in other words, area of the shape plus depth of shape plus

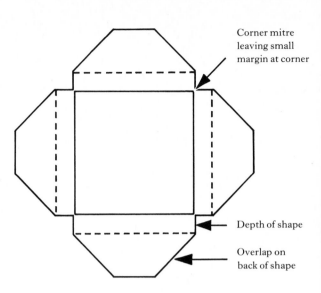

Corner mitre
leaving small
margin at corner

Depth of shape

Overlap on
back of shape

Fig. 4–17. *Method of cutting leather or other fabric being used to cover a square of balsa wood or other foundation material. Measurements should be drawn as accurately as possible.*

Fig. 4–18. *The square base partially covered, showing how the leather has been cut to fit neatly over the wooden base, and then treated with glue.*

amount of overlap on the wrong side. Make sure the overlap is correct; if too little is left it will keep springing up, and if too much is left, it will create an unsatisfactory area in the centre of the shape.

Check the surface of the leather for faults, and check the thickness to find an area which is as thin and as even as possible. Place the foundation shape on the wrong side of the leather in the centre of the chosen area and draw round it carefully. Skiver down the thickness of the leather from the main shape towards the outer edge; use a sharp blade if a skiver knife is not available. (Fig. 4–16.) Cover both surfaces – the top of the foundation shape and the centre area of the leather – with rubber solution, and leave to dry. Place the leather in position, stretching it slightly, and smooth it firmly from the centre towards the edge. Turn it on the wrong side and mark and cut each corner as indicated in the diagram. (Fig. 4–17.) Do not cut directly from the corner, and always allow for the thickness and 'spring' of the leather.

Coat with solution the sides and base of the basic shape and the leather flaps. When dry, ease the leather into place on all sides, stretching it as before to make the shape as neat as possible. (Fig. 4–18.)

Fig. 4-19. *Cardboard shapes prepared with holes punched through each layer, and the anchoring threads in position on the top cardboard shape.*

sides, etc. – keeping them an equal distance from the outer edge. Using a heavy needle or a fine awl, make a hole large enough for a medium-sized threaded needle to pass through. If the shapes are large, make two holes approximately $\frac{1}{4}$ in. (6 mm.) apart at each spot. Place the top shape in position over the next one, and mark the placing of the holes by pushing a needle through the existing ones. Make the holes as before. Continue in this way if there are further layers.

When all the holes have been made, attach the threads to the top shape by using a needle with a double waxed thread, pulling the thread up through one hole and down through the next, leaving approximately 4 in. (96 mm.) lengths of thread hanging on the underside of the shape. Work each pair of holes on the topmost shape in this way. Glue the thread lightly in position on the topside and, if desired, cover the top surface with a layer of felt to conceal the slight bump caused by the thread. (Fig. 4-19.)

Cover the shapes as described before, taking into account the positions of the anchoring threads when finishing the lower side; allow the threads to hang clear by slitting the covering material where necessary.

When each shape is complete, the threads can be taken down through all the matching holes in each successive shape, ending by taking them through the background material in the correct position and finishing them off securely on the wrong side. (Fig. 4-20.)

Many other techniques afford the designer the opportunity to experiment with new methods of working, or to adapt the properties of newly developed materials towards fresh textural results. (Figs. 4-21, 22 and 23; Colour plates 11 and 12.) Exploring the versatility of techniques in this way could result in new variations which, although developed from beginnings rooted in tradition, make a strong original impact.

When covered in this way, the shape must be sewn in position on the background using a glover's needle and the minimum of stitches. In some cases it is not always possible to sew the shape into position, for example, when applying shapes in layers. The following method is a suggestion for overcoming this difficulty.

Cut out the foundation shapes as before and mark specific spots on the top shape – corners, centre of

Fig. 4-20. *The shapes have been covered and the threads taken through the next shape, ready to attach to the background.*

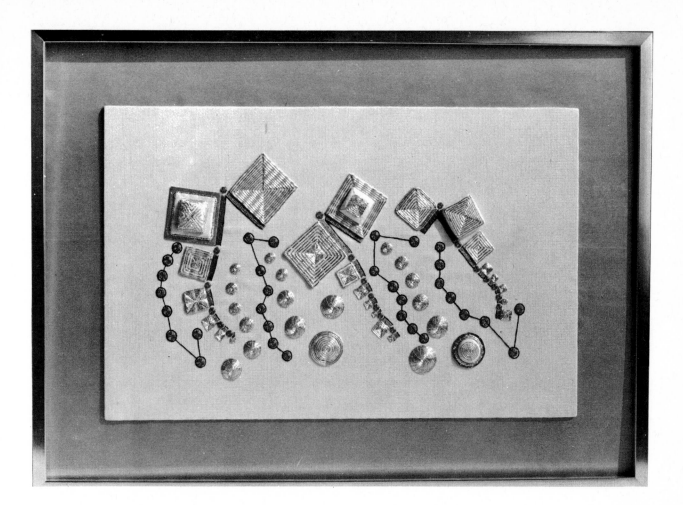

Fig. 4–21. Insect's Legs. *Design developed from analytical drawings of an insect. Tones of grey to black silk on a white silk background, and silver metal thread embroidery. Various techniques are used to create the raised shapes.* Ellen Knap.

Fig. 4–22. *Detail of* Insect's Legs.

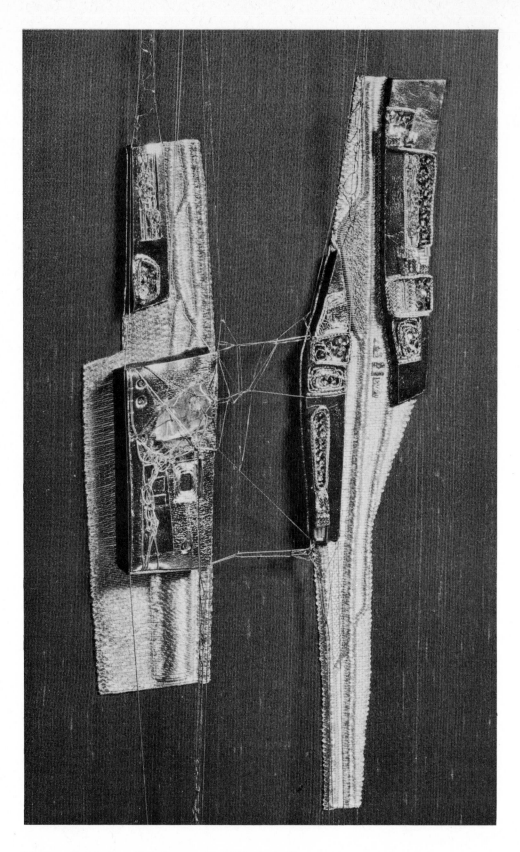

Fig. 4–23. Golden Strata. *Raised areas made of gold leather, gold braids, and beads, creating varied textural surfaces. The large background shapes are worked entirely in laid gold threads, over cords and padding. A piece of amber coloured stone is caught in place by a mesh of gold threads, linking the two main shapes.* (Photograph by Ralph Burnett; property of Miss Margaret Brodie, Architect, Beith.) Hannah Frew.

# 5. Geometric Forms

All things that have life and growth are composed of cell formations or units, carefully organised into systems according to the functional nature of the particular living organism. Nature is the foundation of all geometric systems, and atoms, cells, and groups of cells conform to nature's laws in the formation of all structures, natural and synthetic.

The study of such things as crystals, shells, or snowflakes, shows us the tremendous logic and geometric precision in the formation and arrangement of the individual units involved.

We tend to think of geometry as an academic subject only, and few of us study it at a higher level than in school. However, by taking geometry away from the flat piece of paper we associate it with, and by making use of the theories and methods of producing regular, logical shapes which are its fundamental language, we are shown the way to many forms of three-dimensional expression.

The fascination of geometry grows with deeper study, and while it may be necessary to know a little about the procedure of drawing accurately and measuring angles, etc., it is not essential to be a mathematician to enjoy exploring the visual effects created by geometric shapes and forms.

Various areas of design application make use of geometric developments in their own particular field of study. Packaging and advertising come immediately to mind; interior design is mainly concerned with areas of space enclosed by surfaces; product design with producing forms which have a definite function and an aesthetic quality closely linked with the practical use of the product; architecture with creating space-enclosing structures on a large scale, having a similar aim to that of product design. These and possibly other aspects of design, to a greater or lesser degree, are concerned with the use of geometric shapes and principles.

Architectural forms play a very prominent part in our everyday surroundings, whether we live in cities or in small village communities. We accept the geometric arrangement of walls, floors, ceilings, doors, or windows as a completely natural fact and feel reasonably secure living within them. If the logic of geometry was removed from the planning and construction of buildings, the feeling of security and dependable strength would probably be removed also, although this theory would have to be investigated.

Perhaps it is this sense of security in the logic of geometry that produces a general feeling of enjoyment or satisfaction from a geometric design. Working with and manipulating geometric shapes to produce pattern variations is a fascinating study, and these same simple shapes, when repeated and combined in a pattern or progression, can become the means for building three-dimensional forms. (Fig. 5–1.) Using an equilateral triangle, it is possible to build a regular, spherical shape (icosahedron), provided certain rules are observed (Fig. 5–2.), but it is also interesting to regard the same triangle as a unit with which to produce an irregular surface. (Fig. 5–3.)

Combining two or more geometric shapes extends the possible permutations, the resulting forms becoming more and more complex and intriguing. The common factor linking all these shapes and forms is that they are all composed of faceted surfaces. This immediately involves the aspect of light, which will create interesting tonal effects even when the surfaces are produced in card. The embroiderer can develop this opportunity on textile surfaces, playing with subtle effects such as using different directions of the grain of the fabric, or graded tones, or varied textural finishes, all of which depend on the presence of light to produce their maximum effect. (Colour plate 16.)

It is in the exploration and development of geometric design, more so than in any other form of design, that the effect of 'implied' three-dimensional form can be achieved. (Colour plate 15.) By careful use of colour and tone in relation to the position of the shapes, it is possible to baffle the eye and produce decidedly three-dimensional images on a two-dimensional surface. With the added use of perspective the effects can be quite remarkable. The choice of fabric in

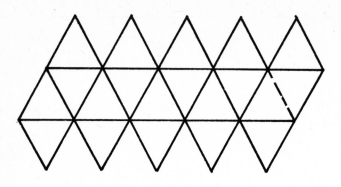

Icosahedron

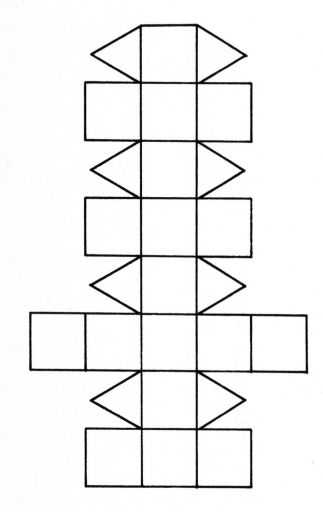

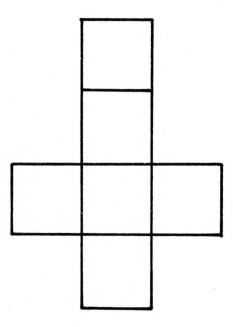

Rhombicuboctahedron or
square-spin

Cube

Fig. 5-1. *The arrangement of geometric forms.*

Snub-dodecahedron

Fig. 5-2. *Examples of spherical forms produced from a logical arrangement of geometric shapes (snub-dodecahedron, icosahedron, and rhombicuboctahedron or square-spin) cut out of cardboard, scored and bent into shape.*

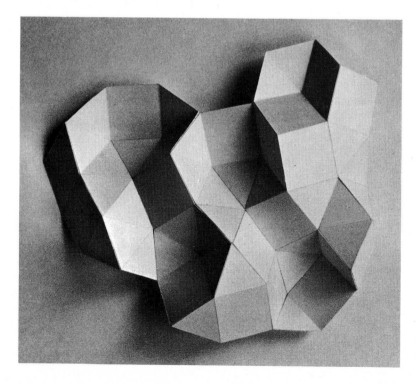

Fig. 5-3. *Squares and triangles combined in a random pattern.*

Fig. 5−4. *Flat patchwork sampler using graded tones of textured materials, giving an illusion of depth.* Mary Pilpak.

Fig. 5−5. Colour Cubes. *Patchwork design based on cubes, making use of both actual and implied three dimensions. The design is carried out in bright, strong colours.* Marion McKay.

51

Fig. 5–6. *Detail of* Colour Cubes.

these designs is extremely important, depending very largely on the tone of colour and the use of the direction of the grain of the fabric to heighten the illusion of depth. (Figs. 5–4, 5 and 6.)

The rather complicated appearance of some of the completed geometric forms may be off-putting to the beginner, but on closer study they are generally found to consist of simple units placed in a regular system or pattern. To start with, a simple cube shape may be made from an arrangement of squares (Fig. 5–7.): draw the squares as accurately as possible on to thin cardboard, using a very sharp, light pencil, and then

cut round the outside edge carefully with a fine, sharp cutting knife and steel rule. Score across the inside lines using the knife and rule, but only cut approximately halfway through the card. This enables the squares to be bent at an angle of 90° to take up the form of a cube. The edges of the cube must be glued together to make a well finished shape, and one method of doing this inconspicuously is to use a quick-drying glue on a small scrap of card, drawing it along the extreme outside edge of the shape. Each edge should be lightly smeared with glue and allowed to dry; when the edges are placed together the glue holds quite firmly. Make a number of

Fig. 5-7. *Cardboard cube. The cut shape, scored and bent ready to glue into shape, is shown next to a completed cube.*

cubes of the same size or varying sizes and build three-dimensional compositions, or combine them with another shape, such as the tetrahedron (Fig. 5-8.), (a four-sided pyramid built with four equilateral triangles), making sure that the sides of the shapes are the same size in order to get the maximum amount of manoeuvrability.

From a simple beginning of this kind one can take a number of different courses:

(a) Study these compositions, and make perspective drawings of them, using tone to heighten the effect of depth. This could then develop into implied three-dimensional design, or by using the resulting shapes it could lead to other ways of producing interesting forms.

(b) Progress from simple geometric structures to more ingenious arrangements, moving away from proven examples and developing freer shapes which produce irregularly faceted surfaces.

(c) Explore further the surfaces of the cube or tetrahedron, scoring and bending to discover other possibilities. This method will produce completely different forms and shapes from any other investigation, and could lead to the combination of straight and curved folds.

Fig. 5–8. *Pyramid shapes which are repeated and combined in a variety of methods.* (Photograph by Francis B. Dunbar, B. Arch., A.R.I.B.A., F.S.A. (Scot.))

Fig. 5–9. *Circles scored and bent to create new forms.* (Photograph by Francis B. Dunbar, B. Arch., A.R.I.B.A., F.S.A. (Scot.)) R. B. Blackburn and Billy West.

Fig. 5–10. Pink to Blue. *Arrangement of geometric shapes in subtle colours, some protruding, some receding, and the remainder flat.* Carolyne Murison.

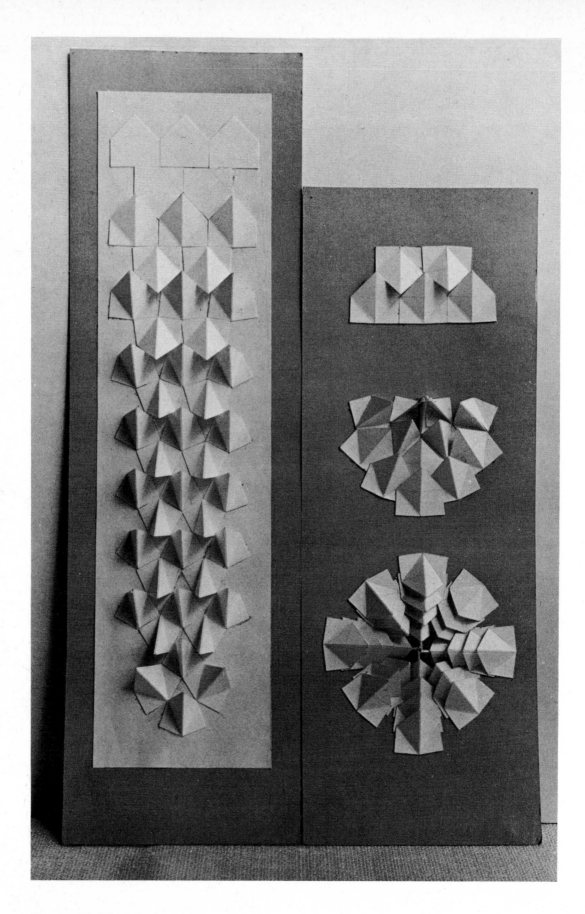

Fig. 5–11. *Work sheets, showing experiments using a simple unit made of thin cardboard*. Carolyne Murison.

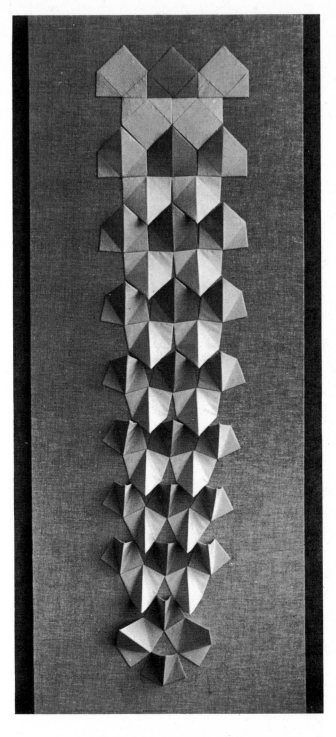

Fig. 5–13. Pendant. *Striped material in graded tones of golden brown over card shapes, with handmade cords and wooden beads interlaced through the open spaces of the geometric design.* Isobel McGregor.

Fig. 5–12. *Development from card experiments, using coloured poplin over card shapes. The three-dimensional element is graded from flat at the top of the panel to deep at the base by increasing the fold on the unit.* Carolyne Murison.

Most geometric designs tend to be derived from straight-edged shapes, but rounded shapes such as circles or cones provide great scope for investigation. (Fig. 5–9 and Colour plate 14.) They tend to be less manageable than flat card, but materials such as acetate, cardboard or plastic tubing, firm plastic, etc. are suitable for trying out ideas. These materials create

suitably tense curves or firm edges as required in formal geometry, and, depending on the investigation and development being carried out, they can either be covered with fabrics to create textural surfaces or used in conjunction with threads. (Figs. 5–10, 11, 12, 13 and 14.)

Solid geometric forms are more readily created,

Fig. 5–14. *Experimental exercise creating a cell-like structure which fits into a right-angled corner.* Isobel McGregor.

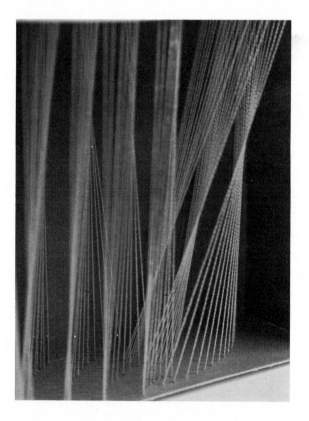

Fig. 5–15. *Experimenting with threads in space, repeating lines making shapes.*

manoeuvred, and composed than implied forms in space, which may be achieved by leading threads across open space to enclose areas in a certain formation. (Figs. 5–15, 16 and 17.) Some examples of this form of design have been produced, but unfortunately the majority have been rather gimmicky and inconclusive. There is room for further investigation of this form which might lead to better and less instant results.

The illusion of threads floating in space to form a regular rounded shape can be created by building the basic shape in a transparent material such as clear acetate or plastic tubing, and organising the threads over the surface. (Fig. 5–18.) Unfortunately, it is not possible to obliterate the light-reflecting quality of these materials, and a highlight always appears when the material is curved. Nevertheless, this method can be a satisfactory way of creating light, open forms moving away from a two-dimensional surface.

Doubtless there are many other avenues of individual exploration to be found in geometric beginnings, besides those mentioned here. It is always possible to go back to the beginning and find new ways for developing ideas, rooted in nature's ingenious formations.

Fig. 5–16. Squares and Rectangles. *Controlled lines of shaded grey threads over silk covered cardboard 'walls', against a background of three different coloured silks. The background silks were used in the construction of the frame.* Ellen Knap.

Fig. 5–17. *Detail of* Squares and Rectangles.

Fig. 5–18. *Work in progress on a small hanging. Various methods of
using threads three-dimensionally are shown: wrapping around perspex
rods, drinking straws and flat ribbons of stiffening, and laying threads over
curved acetate.* Hannah Frew.

# 6. Sources of Inspiration

Space and form are an integral part of existence. Almost everything around us has this quality of taking up a volume of space, making its own characteristic shape, and fitting into a given area. We accept this as a simple fundamental fact, without consciously appreciating the impact that space has on our lives. Perhaps we are now becoming more aware of it, as open space becomes increasingly precious in the face of greater congestion from the large man-made objects which have become so important to modern living. The proportions of solid shape to open space are changing rapidly, and the character and pattern of our towns and cities are becoming almost international, rather than distinctive of an individual country. This is a wide, general view of the use of space in our surroundings, whereas the artist is mainly concerned with a smaller, more concentrated aspect, finding inspiration on a purely personal level.

Drawing is the artist's means of recording impressions and ideas, making marks on paper which represent his own observations of whatever inspires him. The drawing may have one of a number of aims – a straightforward attempt to put on paper a representational image of the object, as an end product (Fig. 6–1.) – a shorthand note of a particular group of shapes for reference (Fig. 6–2.)–or the first stage in discovering shapes and lines which will develop through analysis into design (Figs. 6–3, 4 and 5.) In all of these cases, the artist is faced with the problem of transferring a three-dimensional image on to a two-dimensional surface, and the result depends on the initial inspiration. One person may be inspired by the quality of pattern in a particular area of countryside, while another is excited by the effect of light and shade over the surface of the same area. Each drawing would record the inspirational view of the object, resulting in two completely different statements.

Fig. 6–1. *Fine line drawing of gentians.* Linda Smith.

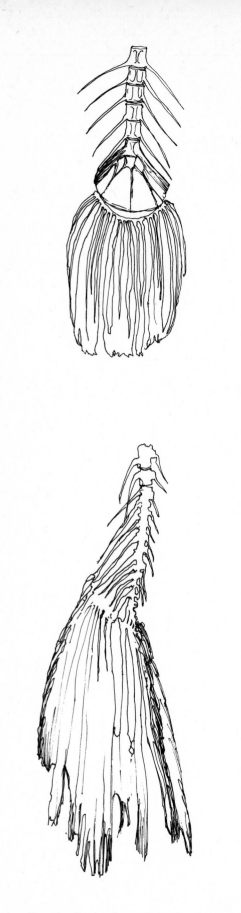

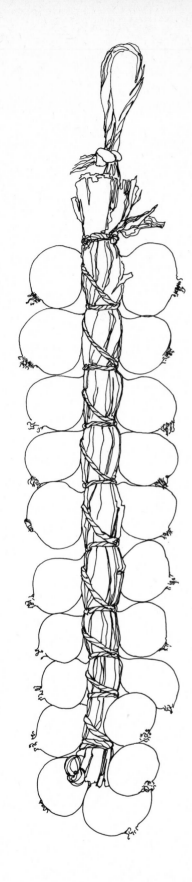

Fig. 6–2. Fins. *Two line drawings exploring the structure of a fin, each using the proportions of heavily jointed structure to finely spaced spines.* Carolyne Murison.

Fig. 6–3. Garlic. *Repetitive forms creating a pattern of smoothly rounded shapes in contrast to the central column of bound linear strands.* Carolyne Murison.

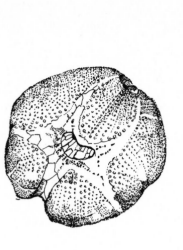

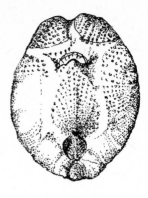

Fig. 6–4. Sea Urchins. *The method employed in drawing these forms helps to portray more clearly the nature and surface of the sea urchins.* Carolyne Murison.

Fig. 6–5. Barnacles. *Interesting possibilities could develop from this drawing, using a variety of techniques and experimenting with different scales of working.* Carolyne Murison.

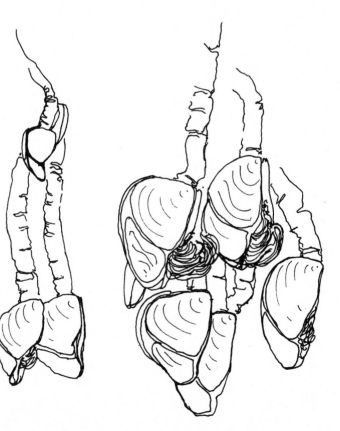

It can be very difficult to transfer our mental vision of a spatial effect on to paper. We have to make do with an unsatisfactory image which has very little of the original impact, and rely to a very great extent on the inner excitement stored in our memory to recreate the vision as we carry out the design. It is probably as important to write notes on observations as to sketch, because very often words can capture an emotion, a colour, or a movement much more realistically than a series of lines or shapes. The combined effect of draw-

ing and writing when the mental image is clear and fresh should be sufficient to conjure up, in retrospect, the original stimulation.

One of the principal factors often involved in the initial stimulus for three-dimensional design is the effect of light and shade on a particular shape or group of shapes. (Figs. 6–6 and 7.) If we can analyse a particular design source into separate areas – such as directions of planes, the main light-catching surfaces, and the degree of form required to convey the subject

Figs. 6−6 and 7. *Rock formations, forming rhythms and patterns.*

(whether it must be completely in the round, bas-relief, or implied three dimensions) – we will move a stage towards linking the original inspiration to a textile reality. (Figs. 6−8 and 9.)

Each person has a purely individual approach to observation and selection; everyone reacts so differently to circumstances, situations, and ideas, that inspiration becomes entirely a private concern. The embroiderer, like any other artist-craftsman, translates mentally into his or her particular medium –

textures, threads, and fabrics – while thinking towards a design expression which stems from the visual or mental stimulus as it is received into the imagination. (Fig. 6−10.)

When working with three-dimensional design, the inspiration for the work must come directly from a three-dimensional source (Figs. 6−11 and 12.) It is not enough to use the third dimension superficially, in the hope of adding some interest to the design; it must be an integrated part of the entire conception of the subject.

Fig. 6–8. *The large enclosing form of a Gunnera-type plant on the shore.*

Fig. 6–9. *Textural free pattern of sawn logs.*

Nature offers us limitless sources for design inspiration in all its aspects, but the study of space is the most important. Everyone finds a degree of fascination, in some cases almost to the point of hypnosis, in watching the surge and flow of water, the steady rhythm of wave after wave rolling into shore in a recurring pattern, as endless as time itself. It is a frustrating though compelling exercise to try to capture the exact shape, form, and movement of a wave. We struggle to note in the mind's eye how the water swells up to form a ridge, changing and growing until it crashes over and is lost in a welter of swirling foam.

How does one then begin to convey the intriguing force of the sea, the movement and flow, the way the light glances off the smooth glassy crest of the ridge? Many different artists have done so, using their own

Fig. 6–10. *The trunk of a palm tree provides inspiration for many textile possibilities, using threads or materials, traditional or original techniques.*

Fig. 6–11. *Light creating gradations and patterns on ripples of water.*

personal forms of expression, with very varied results.

The same kind of fascination is exerted by fire. Everyone has watched a fire at some point in their lives, although a domestic coal fire is now a rare feature. The flames leap up, twisting and coiling round each other, creating rhythms and movements unique to flames. On closer observation, it will be discovered that the flames themselves develop different characteristics according to the substance being burnt. To have spent hours watching a log fire, observing the long, flat tongues of flame licking around the logs, moulding themselves to the surface of the wood, could inspire the designer to apply the basic properties of flames to a purely textile conception, exploiting the movement and pliability

of fabrics in relation to the character of the flames, and resulting in a personal statement about fire. (Colour plate 13.)

Not only can form and movement be seen and be visually exciting, but the sense of touch and feeling can add to the inspiration and interest. The movement of the sea and the effect of waves beating on the shore react on the sand and create little solid ripples or echoes of waves. (Fig. 6–13.) The patterns of sand ridges on a beach are beautiful to look at, as is the iridescent quality of light reflecting on them, but it is also wonderful to walk over them, the feeling of the moving sand underfoot heightening the experience. Pebbles, boulders, and driftwood smoothed by the constant washing

Fig. 6–12. *Lines of laid threads on a grey silk background create an illusion of recession. The firm gauze-like braids looping across the surface are controlled to heighten the impression of perspective.* Fiona Kirkwood.

of the sea demand to be touched as well as looked at, for us to appreciate their qualities fully.

Embroidery has this quality too: a sensitive use of textural surfaces which intensifies the tactile effect of the design, and helps to emphasise the original impact of the inspiration, especially when applied to three-dimensional work.

Purely imaginative concepts and ideas can lead to design expressions which must be stated in terms of three dimensions. The natural force of wind, for instance, and the mental images it evokes, take on a depth and power which require stronger definition than two-dimensional statements. Wind can only be observed through its effect on objects, although it is possible

that we subconsciously relate the element with the shapes it makes. So, when we use them to express the abstract idea, the visible result is an intermingling of imagination and effect. (Fig. 6–14.)

Abstract ideas, coming as they do purely from the imagination of the artist and involving the expression of emotions rather than facts, have to be turned over in the mind thoroughly in order to clarify the true intention of the resulting statement. The original excitement must remain clear, but ideas have to be sifted out to eliminate distractions. Mental images must become actual images through an intermediate process which blends intuitive creation with skilful designing. The true success of the result can be judged by the artist

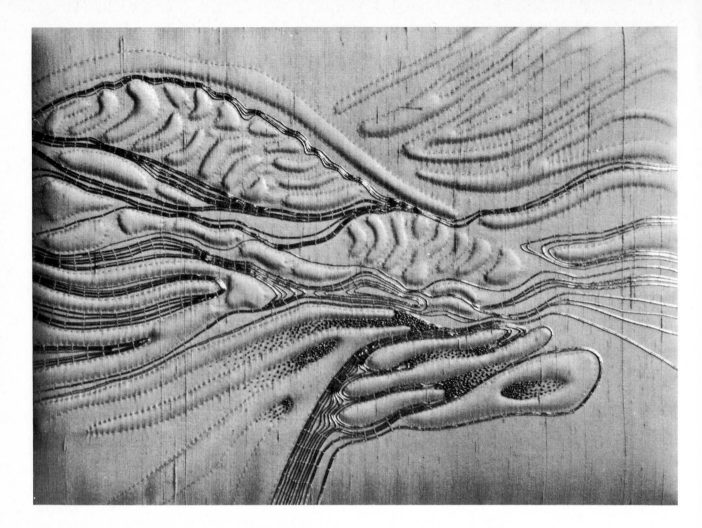

Fig. 6–13. Sand Ripples *(see Colour plate 4)*. *Corrugations created by the movement of waves over sand, highlighted and accentuated by the flow of water around them.* Christine Simpson.

alone, since all other reactions to the statement are based on the viewer's personal feelings, and lack the experience of the original stimulation.

The embroiderer experiences tremendous enthusiasm and excitement when involved with materials and threads, just as any other artist is motivated and excited by contact with their particular medium. This feeling is very personal, concerning only the artist-designer and the qualities contained in the material.

The initial desire to use a particular thread or material determines the method of using it and the means of conveying a particular textile idea. Take, for instance, a beautiful shot silk with the lovely crisp, crackly feeling that is typical of certain silks. The use of

it would involve both exploiting the colour properties by altering the direction of the grain of the material, and searching for that essence of crispness in a subject matter which included shapes and forms able to express the original reaction to the material.

In the same way, a certain embroidery technique may be the starting point for an idea, and would be the basis for subsequent developments, each stage or thought referring to the main source of inspiration for its existence. A technique such as smocking, which makes use of the effect of drawing up material into folds and using the folds as a foundation on which to work, could be the starting point for a design idea. The application of this technique has become linked

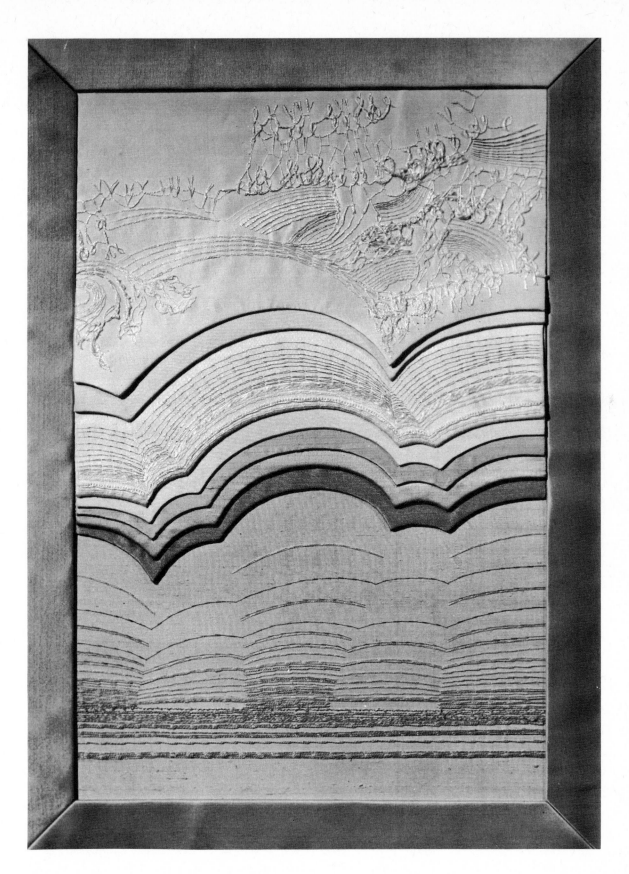

Fig. 6–14. Mistral. *Design inspiration from the movement and rhythm of the wind. The slow, warm, gentle breeze at the bottom of the design swells and strengthens into recurring 'gusts', and results in swirling movement at the top.* (Photographic Department, Glasgow School of Art; property of Mrs N. Bergh, New York.) Hannah Frew.

Fig. 6–15. *Detail of* Golden Disc *(see Colour plate 12). A double investigation, involving colour progression and the three-dimensional use of goldwork. The visual means of expressing the colour theme emerged as a simple chequerboard arrangement. This in turn became the grid through which a golden disc protruded, being background level at the outer edge and becoming progressively deeper towards the centre. The completed embroidery was stretched over board tensed into a curve; this emphasised the aim of the work, which was to give greater play of light to the colour gradations, and exaggeration of height to the three-dimensional theme.* (Property of Mr and Mrs H. J. White, New York.) Hannah Frew.

almost exclusively to children's clothes, blouses, etc. and has not been investigated sufficiently as a free means of expressing movement in materials. The rhythm of folds catching the light and creating ripple effects could become the basis for an imaginative composition, combining the technical skill of the embroiderer with the essential qualities of pliability and surface texture contained in materials. Certain embroidery stitches are traditionally used to create pattern allied to the regular folds, organised by the careful gathering of the foundation material. Other stitches, though, could also be introduced, or there might be no obvious stitching at all, only subtle control of the material,

in order to exploit this technique to its fullest extent.

Source material can be as wide or as narrow as each individual requires. (Figs. 6–15, 16 and 18.) One artist may feel she needs the whole range of visual stimulus in order to explore and develop ideas, finding starting points in each working area which direct her exploration on to another field of study; another artist will make it her life-time's single project to develop and investigate one subject area and all its ramifications. Each individual finds his or her own particular channel of inspiration and can be fired with enthusiasm for a subject in a purely personal way, involving no one else and affecting no other person in exactly the same way.

Fig. 6–16. Cycles. *This panel is the final work on the theme of 'Cycles' which arose from an investigation into a project based on 'Living Design'. The significance of cycles relating to the working of human bodies, vegetation, natural forces, etc., and the fact that cycles are interdependent in maintaining life, led to the search for a symbol with which to state this theme in design terms.*

*The original unit was a strip of paper, which was twisted and then joined to form a circular loop. More units were constructed and intertwined in order to create more complicated modules. These were then photographed to facilitate the study of the resulting shapes and patterns.*

*The most simple module was selected for its impact and enlarged to a more sympathetic scale, using both actual and implied three-dimensional effects.* Margaret Hinshaw.

Fig. 6–17. *Design units produced in strips of paper, interlaced and combined in various compositions.* (Photographic Department, Glasgow School of Art.)

Fig. 6–18. *Detail of* Cycles. *Silk shapes and silk stitchery are used on
the background; graded tones and the direction of the stitchery create an
illusion of depth. Stiffened silk shapes, arched and intertwined, give
strong definition to the design.* Margaret Hinshaw.

# 7. Design

The original excitement of an idea is the spark that sets off the desire to design, to produce in a visual statement the whole thought and inspiration that comes from within the artist. The first step can be daunting, as there can be a jealous fear of making that statement about a secret thought, of revealing one's personal ideas to the possible criticism of others. It is only through reflection that they can grow and develop into tangible works, and become not only the artist's thoughts in actual form but extensions of these thoughts, through the development of sensitivity to textile materials.

The actual process of designing really becomes a series of decisions taken by the designer as each situation presents itself. More often than not, the choice to be made is not between a right and a wrong move, but to select one of a great many subtle variations. The final choice depends on the designer's personal, intuitive appreciation and consciousness of basic design principles.

Before actually beginning to make any statement, it is essential to think 'through' the subject thoroughly, to be ruthless about the aim of the design, and to set out, in order, exactly what is required of the finished work. In other words, once the main theme of the work is established firmly at the beginning everything that follows will work towards it.

One of the first decisions to be made is how the idea is going to be portrayed, whether it will be completely in three-dimensional form, standing or hanging free; if it will be a more conventional arrangement on a background; or something completely different from any of these basic beginnings. (Figs. 7–1 and 2.) The next deciding factor will be the scale of the design, since so many other factors will be dependent upon it.

The choice of scale in which to present the original thought will depend, to a great extent, on the kind of impact intended, or upon the nature of the inspiration. For instance, the designer's imagination may have been fired by the intricacies of a particular flower head, and she may be inspired to represent the flower visually,

attempting to emphasise the shapes and spaces produced by the growth and development of that particular species. (Fig. 7–3.) In doing so, one has the choice of portraying it either as a fine, rich, delicate piece of embroidery on a small scale, or deliberately enlarging it to many times its normal size to surprise the viewer and exaggerate the form. (Colour plates 18, 19, and 20.)

If the size chosen is very large, then the original design statement has to be carried out on a smaller scale, for purely practical reasons. Half or quarter size would generally be suitable, since it is fairly easy to enlarge from these, but this depends also on the materials being used to carry out the mock-up. When it is necessary to make a trial mock-up, it is advisable to try out a small section of the design full size, in order to make it 'real' enough to see what has to be tackled. A design changes drastically when blown up to several times its original size, and very often preconceived ideas must undergo considerable rethinking.

Closely linked with scale is the subject of proportion. Proportions of shapes to background, shapes to lines, amount of one colour to another, one tone to another, one texture to another, occur in every design (Fig. 7–4.), but in our particular study of the third dimension, the balance between flat to rounded, thin to thick, becomes extremely important and will differentiate between a good design and an unsatisfactory one. (Fig. 7–5.)

Size is an essential part of everything, and the size of one object relates to the sizes around it. If there is no obvious or considered relationship, then the eye is confused and uncertain. For example, a photograph of a piece of rock could be either a huge boulder or a small pebble enlarged, unless something is included to indicate scale, such as a human figure or a hand. Certain sizes and amounts co-exist happily and create a sense of mutual belonging and easy acceptance, while others may be unbalanced and produce a feeling of tension or uneasiness. This can be readily observed in everyday things around us – plants in flower pots for example.

Fig. 7–1. *Drawing of corn, using various media and exploring the linear quality of the leaves in contrast to the corn.* Margaret McFedries.

soft, padded shapes.
bold geometric patterns.
patchwork, applique?
totem pole appearance

Fig. 7–2. *Design ideas which developed from the drawings of corn.*
Margaret McFedries.

Fig. 7–3. *Detail of* Orchids *(see Colour plate 18). Areas of the design
develop naturally from the original drawing into stitchery and laid metal
thread work. The third dimension emerges gradually from the background
in leaf shapes and coiling stems, culminating in the intricately formed
flower head.* Lindsay Hoyle.

Fig. 7–4 *(see Colour plate 2)*. Landscape. *Carefully considered proportions of stripes, colour, and texture, with the strong contrast of smoothly curving tubes. 36 × 42 ins. (91·5 × 107 cm.)* Mary Gribble.

Fig. 7–5. Water-lily Roots. *Machine-embroidered panel showing
gradual change of size and scale of working to create a feeling of depth.
27 × 56 ins. (68·5 × 142 cm.)* Jennifer Wilson.

Fig. 7—6. *Designing with material : exploring the possibilities of producing a three-dimensional thread design.* Christine Simpson.

Fig. 7—7. *Another experiment using fabric as the design medium.* Margaret Lane.

If the plant has grown too large for the pot, the mass of foliage and flower will overwhelm the pot and produce an uneasy feeling that the slightest touch will physically overbalance the entire plant. On the other hand, a large plant pot containing a small plant or seedling will give the plant a ridiculous appearance, while making the plant pot look much heavier than it really is.

Observation, experiment, and practice help the designer find the answer to problems of proportion (Figs. 7—6, 7 and 8); but while there may be certain basic directives towards producing good proportion, each design situation demands a fresh look at the subject.

Generally the most interesting and intriguing designs are extremely successful because of an unusual or clever approach to proportion, where the designer has taken a chance and experimented with quantities to produce a tantalising balance, rather than a safe, con-

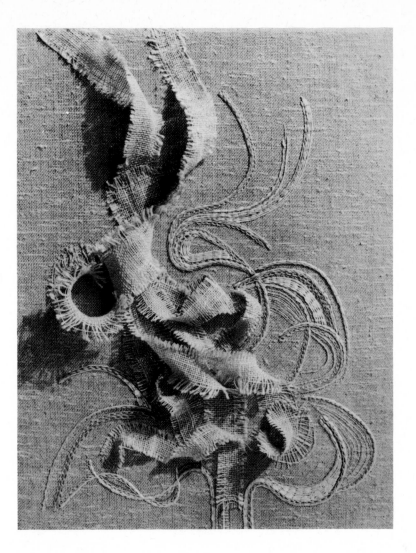

Fig. 7–8. *Small experimental panel using raw-edged strips of linen, echoed in lines of stitchery.* Sandra McLeod.

ventional result. The rules are made to be broken, with unhappy results nine times out of ten, but occasionally an outstanding design will be created which owes its brilliance to experiment. It is in the handling of proportion and contrast that a designer can produce the maximum impact from the ingredients she holds, both by using the imagination to produce an original approach, and in the skilful application of fundamental design principles.

When dealing with three-dimensional design in this context, the danger is overstatement. The subject matter and the aim of the designer dictate the amount of modelling required to carry out the design. If the dimension is overstated the result will be heavy and cumbersome. Padding out a particular area of a design gives it emphasis, which is the intention of the designer, but great care must be taken to ascertain that when combined with colour and texture this emphasis does not degenerate into vulgarity. (Colour plates 17 and 23.)

Not only the amount of depth should be considered

at this point, but also the method of building the three-dimensional areas. The subject may call for a raised, rounded effect in the final arrangement, but the choice will be either to create a solid, padded area or a more open, lighter, curved surface, either of which may be the answer. These factors become more obvious as the designer begins to build the ideas with actual materials.

This first step towards creating a finished work should be as fluid as possible. Initially, a variety of approaches or arrangements may be in the designer's mind; consequently, a method by which the various shapes or components of the design can be easily built or mass-produced is a decided advantage. Ingenuity comes into its own here, when the search for a manipulative medium leads one to experiment with various items, such as hair clips, ping-pong balls, egg boxes, etc. Some experiment and invention at this stage can enable the designer to adapt or manoeuvre the various parts of the design into compositions which would not otherwise have been considered or even thought of.

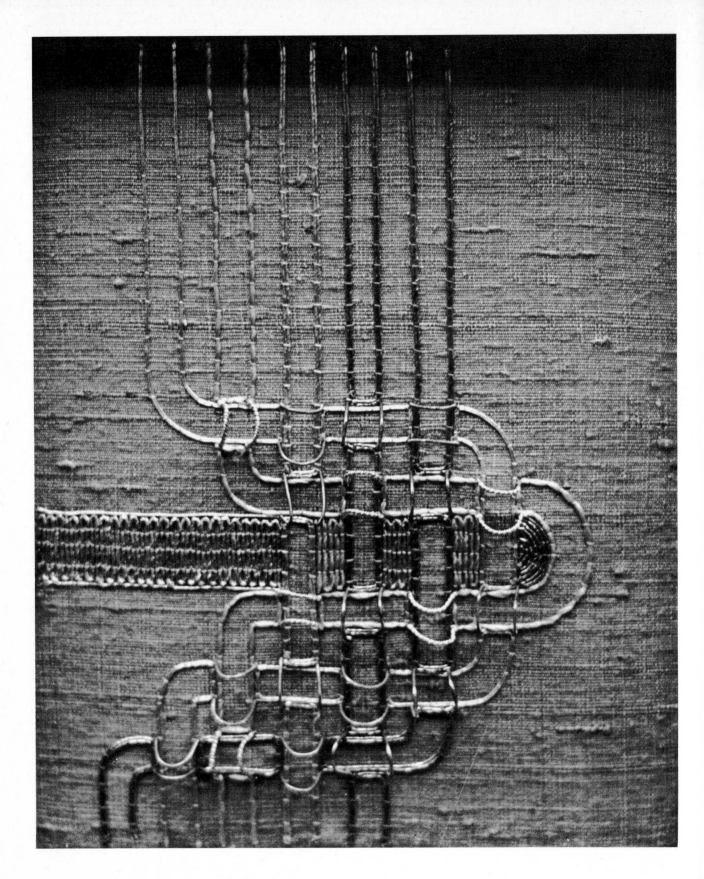

Fig. 7–9. Interwoven Theme. *Small panel of laid thread work,*
*illustrating the use of lines in design, creating paths for the eye to follow.*
$8\frac{1}{2} \times 10$ *ins. (22 × 25·5 cm.)* Linda Drummond.

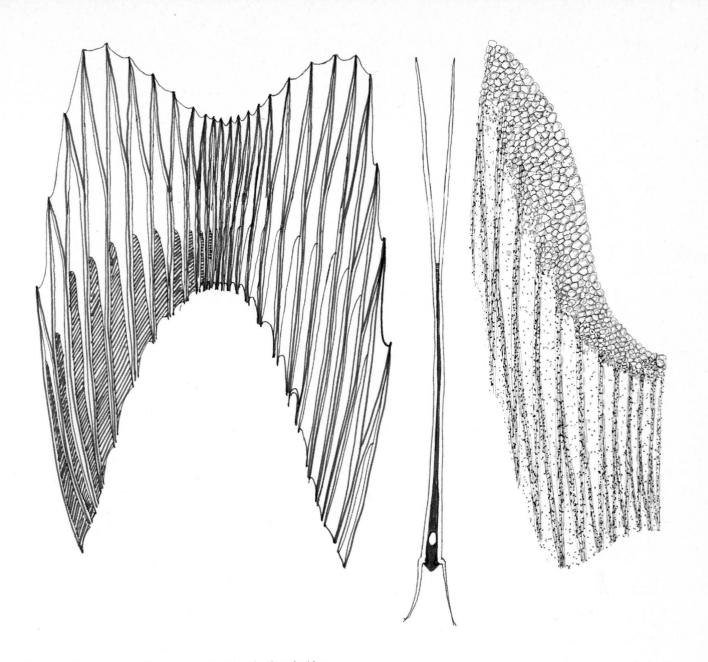

Fig. 7–10. *Drawing of a fish fin, from which the design for the embroidery was taken.* Rita Winters.

Through handling these experimental materials, other design possibilities may present themselves. It may be easier to represent a large raised area by devising a series of units linked or joined together; in doing so, it may be found that the area has become much more interesting through the introduction of repetitive pattern.

In some cases, it is very difficult to devise a convincing mock-up, but no matter how unfinished or raw the result may appear it is of immense value in this intermediate stage. Padded areas can be constructed by crushing up tissue paper, gluing it lightly in position, and then covering it either with flat tissue paper, folded and tucked over the basic shape, or with one or more layers of scrim. Either of these surfaces can be painted afterwards to get the effect of colour and tone on the raised area. Moulded plastic holders for sweets, biscuits, etc. can be used as building material, either whole or shredded to create raised textural surfaces.

Cardboard is excellent for scoring and bending, either for rounded or angular designs, but may begin to crack and fold if too much pressure is applied. Cords, string, cotton wool, steel wool, foam rubber, Polystyrene, plastic sheet or tubing, scraps of machinery, anything expendable that has form will help towards assembling an opening statement. Having fun with the materials at this stage teaches us a great deal about producing three-dimensional forms, and will be of

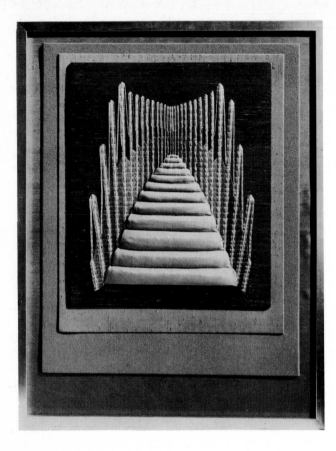

Fig. 7–11. Fish Fin. *Panel of laid thread techniques carefully planned in a gradation of size and tone, using grey silk and silver on a stepped background of tones of dull pink. The raised area is made of quilted grey silk. 25 × 32 ins. (64 × 82 cm.)* Rita Winters.

Fig. 7–12. *Detail of* Fish Fin.

great assistance when the design is actually being carried out in the chosen fabrics.

When the various components of the design have been collected, no matter how roughly, the vital decision of making a telling composition with them begins to assail the designer. It must be a similar mental experience to that of the conductor of an orchestra, who has all the basic components already there, but who depends on his control and handling of those components for success.

From the very first positioning of one shape on to a background, a relationship is set up between the positive (solid shape) and negative (open surrounding space) which now becomes the focal point for the designer's concentration. With the addition of further shapes, lines, or masses, this relationship becomes more intricate, always needing careful observation to ensure that the background does not become a conglomeration of broken up areas with no reference to each other. The eye moves around a design according to the path set out by the designer. (Fig. 7–9.) It can move more slowly and easily if the placing of the shapes has been controlled in that way, or it can be given a series of shock moves, intended by the artist to provide an exciting experience for the viewer. If, however, the composition has not been considered in this way, if it has been dealt with superficially, without thought being given to the relationship between all the various parts, the visual appraisal of the design will be jumbled, uncertain, and disturbing.

Returning to the analogy of orchestral music, the parallel here would be in the appreciation of quiet passages and silent pauses in relation to strong, swelling crescendoes of sound, or the crashing chords which give contrast and excitement to the senses by their sheer unexpectedness, all adding up to a pleasurable variation within the composition.

An imbalance of shape to background, or raised surface to flat, will produce a feeling of monotony, overweight, or sparseness and a general lack of excitement. Shapes, lines, and masses are foils to each other, accentuating their inherent characteristics when sensitively used and sympathetically observed by the designer.

The initial design may go through various stages of development as the inspiration begins to take shape and form; additional influences create new circumstances for the designer to assess, either to accept or reject.

Some design ideas call for more design preparation than others, and in certain cases the embroiderer may feel the need to by-pass this initial design stage altogether, and set to work immediately with materials and threads. Generally, however, it is more satisfactory to try out ideas on paper first (Fig. 7–10.), giving oneself the opportunity to adjust thoughts, manipulate shapes, lines, areas, and depth and reach a stage where the fundamental composition can be established as a guide towards the finished design. (Figs. 7–11 and 12.)

# 8. Application of Design

The act of producing a finished embroidery is the culmination of all the designer's study, together with awareness of materials, techniques, and effects, and her experience and skill in handling them.

As in all forms of embroidery, the initial ideas, drawings, and designs are merely stages towards the final statement in fabric and threads. This final stage grows and changes with the introduction of texture and surface effects. As the materials begin to determine various aspects of the work, the design develops and adapts to them.

All previous design attempts can only be used as pointers towards a means of expressing an idea. They serve the very useful purpose of showing in a tangible way the direction in which the designer's thoughts lie. Having made a mock-up version of the mental image, the embroiderer is now able to analyse more easily the main aim of the design and make adjustments and improvements towards that end. It is very easy to become attached to a definite idea which one has nursed through the early stages and carefully developed in design form, and then be reluctant to admit that it is not the best means of conveying the basic message. One must, however, be strong enough to set it aside and search for an alternative solution.

A great deal of time can be spent on initial design ideas and on the refinement of a composition, until eventually the mock-up version of the design becomes a very finished and pleasing piece of work. But it is never possible to go ahead on the assumption that the final work can be an exact rendering of that design. The mock-up is produced in materials such as paper, card, paint, etc. which can never truly express the inherent qualities of fabrics and threads, and as soon as one begins to work with these materials, the character and feeling of the design changes completely. So it is much more fruitful to produce a few rough ideas, indicating different versions of a thought, than to become over-involved in one beautifully finished conception which may not achieve the desired effect.

It is always an excellent idea to remind oneself of the stages previously encountered in resolving various problems, for, while the problems may have taken on a different slant, a backward look can often help to clarify the situation and remind one of the basic requirements set down at the start. Having made that statement, it must be kept in mind that from now on, during the execution of the work, the decisions must refer only to the final stage of the embroidery, by which the success of the work will be judged.

One of the main ingredients of three-dimensional embroidery is the effect of light on the textural surfaces. Here again, the choice of fabric determines the way in which the composition will react, and only by experimenting with textures within the arrangement can the embroiderer decide on the most effective use of the materials within the design. (Fig. 8–1.) This is one reason why it is imperative for the designer to keep an open mind about the final appearance of the work, and be ready to adapt and translate the composition as the work develops.

The appearance of three-dimensional compositions may vary greatly according to the direction of the light source. When the light source changes, the highlights on the raised areas change also, not only in their placing but in shape and intensity. Light creates lines, spots, flat facets, or diffused areas according to the character of the shapes and textures being used, and these form associated compositions to be considered in addition to the main design composition. It becomes a complex but fascinating occupation to deal with these permutations of light patterns and to consider their possibilities within a design.

Materials have been discussed in a previous chapter, where their qualities and properties were examined in a fairly general way, but at this stage their observation and use is more specific. Each area becomes not just a point of interest in its own right but part of a complex and sensitive composition of textile shapes, dependent on each other to produce an over-all textural effect. (Figs. 8–2, 3, 4 and 5.)

The characteristics of individual materials should be

Fig. 8–1. Red Wall. *The importance of proportion in design is illustrated here by the balance of sizes of stripes, and the amounts of textural treatment.* 50 × 60 ins. (127 × 152 cm.) Jennifer Hex.

Fig. 8–2. *Detail of* Nursery Panel *(see Colour plate 17)*. *Striped cotton, felt, seersucker, and other fabrics are used to produce colourful flower shapes*. Marion MacKay.

emphasised and used fully to give expression to the work. When used three-dimensionally these characteristics become even more obvious and need to be used positively in relation to the design. For instance, a material such as corded velvet has a strong directional quality, and when used over a curving surface the parallel lines of the fabric exaggerate the curve by intro-

ducing perspective. Lines act as roads leading the eye in a certain direction within a composition, and when the lines are repeated regularly, such as in the weave of corded velvet, the direction indicated becomes more important. These considerations are consistent throughout the final stages of the embroidery, each area being as important as its neighbour, whether it is a focal point

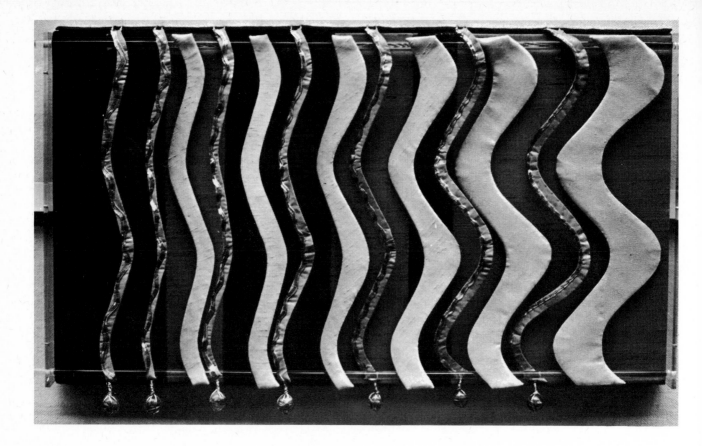

Fig. 8–3. Parlour Game. *A background of stripes provides a static effect as a foil to the curving bands of silk and embroidered silk, which may be adjusted and moved on their perspex rods to produce further permutations and designs. 16 × 30 ins. (41 × 76 cm.)* Kathleen Whyte.

in the design or a background area leading towards it.

Colour used within the composition acquires various additional aspects when allied to a three-dimensional surface. Not only does the embroiderer choose certain colours and tones with which to work, but she has the added bonus of changes of colour and tone produced by an irregular surface. Light affects colour in the round by adding light and depth to tone as well as by diluting or intensifying the colour. When colours are placed beside each other on a flat surface, an optical effect is created by their relationship to each other. For instance, pure red and green will produce a dazzle effect, whereas orange and red will merge together where they meet. An illusion of the third dimension can be made by experimenting with opposite colours, or making use of warm and cool colours with particular attention being paid to the tonal values.

When colours are actually being used over three-dimensional surfaces they also reflect on each other according to their positioning, and this in turn creates another area for investigation of colour with texture. (Colour plate 24.)

Colour theories certainly go a long way towards teaching one what to expect when working with specific colours, but the actual experience of handling materials with their complexity of surfaces and tones provides a wider and more exciting education on the subject. By working constantly with fabrics and threads and trying all kinds of unlikely permutations, even the most experienced embroiderer or designer can find new, surprising colour combinations. (Colour plate 21.)

The choice of foundation materials may also bring a variation to the preconceived ideas of the design. These unseen materials, too, impose their characteristics on the composition, for their individual behaviour affects the appearance of the finished raised areas. For example, plastic tubing has a natural curve which is rather difficult to straighten completely; the embroiderer should therefore accept this curving characteristic and use it constructively, rather than force the

Fig. 8–4. Flo. *Decorative wall hanging, making full use of varied,
printed fabrics in a repeating unit. The padded shapes create an interesting
composition of light and shade. 36 × 72 ins. (91·5 × 183 cm.)*
Marilyn McGregor.

Fig. 8–5. *Detail of* Flo.

Fig. 8–6. Cross Currents. *Design based on the rhythmical movements of water. Different gauges of polythene tubing, covered with silk materials, produce the repeating patterns of water currents. Contrast is provided by free stitchery in silk threads, enclosing pieces of shisha glass and thin slices of polythene tubings. Note the natural curve of the tubing.* (Property of the County Council of Dunbarton Education Department.) Hannah Frew.

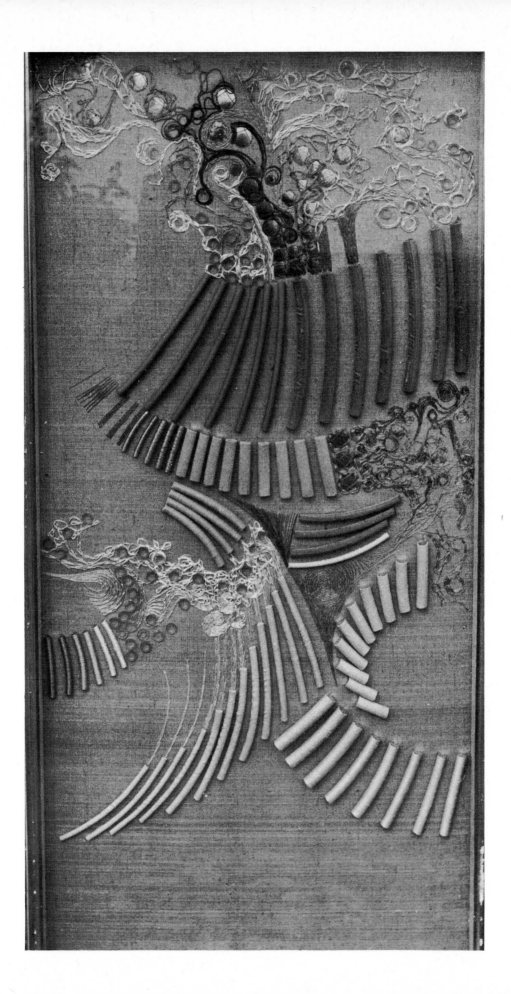

Fig. 8–7. *Detail of* Cross Currents.

Fig. 8–8. Blue Orchid. *Small panel using fine silk fabrics and stitchery.*
*The decorative frame completes the composition and creates balance in*
*the proportions.* Mary Wallace.

tubing to behave in an unnatural manner. (Figs. 8–6 and 7.) The entire feeling of a design may be altered in this way.

Actually working with materials and threads and producing a design using textured three-dimensional surfaces is an exciting and extremely satisfying experience. The richness and stimulation inherent in embroidery give the designer the impetus and excitement with which to carry through a piece of work using colour, texture, and pattern to the fullest advantage. (Colour plate 22.)

Probably one of the most difficult decisions for the embroiderer to make is to determine exactly when to stop. The excitement of a piece of work, plus the sheer pleasure of physically working with threads and materials, makes one reluctant to bring the creative process to an end. The discerning designer realises the value of proportion throughout, and by continually studying the work from a reasonable viewing distance the correct balance can be achieved. It is very important to stand back from the work occasionally, and to see it from the observer's view rather than that of the embroiderer, which is very close. A successful embroidery will always exhibit both qualities: general impact from a distance, and detailed textural interest on closer inspection.

## MOUNTING AND PRESENTATION

Having successfully reached the stage of putting the final touches to the work, it is all too easy to neglect or be unaware of the importance of finish and presentation. Even the most beautifully executed embroidery can appear mediocre, if proper care is not taken to mount it neatly and accurately and to present it appropriately. If the design has been created on a flat background, the work should be stretched carefully over a backing which is firm enough to take the strain, so that the background material is as smooth as possible and the grain of the fabric is parallel to the straight edge of the mount. If it is a three-dimensional object, then every aspect of it should be finished to a professional standard, and sufficient care and attention paid to the way it will hang or stand.

Three-dimensional objects must have this professionalism, as poor presentation distracts attention from the main theme of the design. It is worth taking the trouble to search for items such as nylon filament, which is strong though transparent, for hanging an item unobtrusively; or the correct type of rod with which to support a hanging – for instance, stainless steel, brass, or perspex – rather than making do with any odd piece of wood. In certain cases, wood may be the appropriate material to use, but it must be the right kind of wood, the correct weight, and finished properly. Any material being used as an adjunct or accessory to the embroidery must be considered as carefully as the work itself, and must be handled with the same care and attention to detail and finish.

When the embroidery is presented on a flat, stretched background, consider the design carefully and discover whether it looks complete on its own or if it will be improved by being mounted. The choice of mount to be used becomes part of the designing process. Colour and texture surrounding the embroidered design can alter its balance and appearance, so great care should be taken to select exactly the right tone of colour and the surface quality required to enhance the embroidery.

The mounted panel may need framing, but again this decision depends on the over-all effect of the work and whether visually it needs a frame to contain the design and complete the composition. (Fig. 8–8.) The choice of frame moulding is important: it requires the same careful attention to colour, texture, and proportion as every other part of the design. It need not necessarily be a manufactured frame. If it is difficult to find the right moulding for the panel, it may be that it requires a frame with a textile surface. This can be produced quite simply: cut a firm cardboard shape for each side, mitre the corners, and allow enough depth for the side edge and sufficient overlap for the back (which must be mitred also). Cover the pieces individually with the selected fabric, before joining them at the corners. Then fix the embroidery into the frame and secure it firmly on the wrong side.

The process of finishing must be considered afresh for every design; each piece of work creates its own requirements and must be considered in its own context.

# 9. Embroidery for Specific Situations

A commission to produce a piece of work, either for a private individual or a public body, immediately introduces a feeling of purpose into the act of creating a design. The design has to be worked for a specific reason, and will be placed in a particular setting. While this in itself may impose certain limitations on the embroiderer, there is also the compensating factor that the content of the design is determined from the outset.

The designer's task is to consider all the limitations, study the reasons for the design and the message it is to convey, and develop a sympathetic attitude leading to total involvement. (Figs. 9–1 and 2.)

The obvious restrictions, instead of being inhibiting as they may at first appear, can force the embroiderer to extend beyond herself to produce a more exciting and original answer than would have resulted without them.

Usually the embroiderer is carrying out work whose source was in her own imagination; the work is executed in materials and threads to the designer's own satisfaction, and probably presented for exhibition to the general public. When the original instigation comes from some other source, the direction and emphasis alter in a subtle way to include the desire to please this particular person or group of people and to meet the requirements set down by them.

To begin with, it is important that embroiderer and client should discuss fully every aspect of the commission, so that a complete understanding is established between them. This should include not only the financial and material aspects, but the significance of the design content; both parties should be aware of each other's approach to the subject. There must be a

Fig. 9–1. Storks Flying in the Dawn. *Panel designed to hang in the entrance to the special care unit of a maternity hospital. The aim is to divert the attention of anxious fathers, giving the impression of being cheerful, light-hearted, and calm. 72 × 24 ins. (183 × 61 cm.)* (Photographic Department, Glasgow School of Art; property of the Queen Mother's Hospital, Glasgow.) Kathleen Whyte.

Fig. 9–2. *Detail of* Storks Flying in the Dawn. *Methods of working include quilting in various materials on the storks; and the rays of the rising sun are done as free-hanging flags.*

sympathetic balance between the needs of the client and the embroiderer's freedom to express those needs in design terms.

One of the first things the embroiderer must do when carrying out a commissioned work is to visit the place for which it is being designed, or become familiar with the setting through studying photographs. If it is a church or other public building, the internal proportions of the architecture will be the principal factor governing the general atmosphere. The impression may be of a very high, narrow area within which everything accentuates the loftiness of the building; or there may be a very definite horizontal or diagonal break in the height, such as a gallery or staircase, which will alter the proportions and introduce a different set of directions for the eye to follow. On the other hand, the setting may be on a more domestic level: here the scale will be dif-

ferent again, and the architectural impression may be more horizontal, as in a hospital corridor for instance.

Another important factor to be taken into account is the light source and the way in which the light will be directed on to the embroidery. Very often the positioning of windows in a church or large public building creates an almost theatrical effect of light and shade, and this could be used to the maximum benefit of the design. (Colour plate 27.)

A situation which requires strong impact, such as a pulpit fall for a church, provides an opportunity to use three-dimensional design to its fullest effect. (Colour plate 26.) Light directed on to a raised area accentuates the design by highlighting the outline of the shapes in sharp contrast to the shadows thrown on to the background. An embroidery produced in strong relief 'reads' more easily in a large area than one which is

Fig. 9–3. Animal, Vegetable and Mineral. *This panel was designed to hang in a corridor leading to a hospital lounge. It depicts the growth and development of life in humans and animals on the left panel; strata and crystal formations of minerals in the centre; and cell formations and growth of vegetation on the right. The two outer panels are raised above the level of the central panel, with figures spanning the space to indicate man's involvement with all forms of life and growth.* 36 × 50 ins. (*91·5 × 127 cm.*) (Photographic Department, Glasgow School of Art; property of the Queen Mother's Hospital, Glasgow.) Hannah Frew.

completely flat. This use of the third dimension in embroidery is probably the most satisfying of all, as it fulfils a very definite function, both practically and aesthetically.

When preparing initial ideas to present to the client for approval, it is advisable to have a number of designs from which to choose, and to make the mock-ups as interesting as possible. The embroiderer is well aware of the transformation the design undergoes when it is translated into embroidery, but the layman is probably less informed. A selection of material and thread samples attached to the design mock-up will help the client to form a more definite impression of how the finished work will appear.

There may be slight reluctance on the part of the client to accept the possibilities of three-dimensional work at this early stage, on the grounds of impractic-ability. It is therefore particularly important to present these ideas in as exciting a way as possible, to justify and prove the advantages of this bolder working method.

Colour is an important factor when design ideas are being prepared for a certain place, since the finished work must be considered in relation to the surrounding colours which will influence it. The colours used in the design can either provide a sharp contrast creating a strong focal point, or they can merge and blend with the existing colours. It might be valuable to introduce colour links with definite permanent features, stained glass windows for example, or to provide an interesting contrast of colour which will not depend too heavily on an existing and possibly temporary setting.

The size of the design is determined by the place in which it will be hung. The proportion and shape will be influenced by the surrounding sizes and shapes. This in turn will help to determine methods and materials used.

A specific intention underlies each individual commission, no matter whether it is destined for church, council chamber, or private home. It conveys a message, or has some other reason for existence, and the design must indicate this clearly. When designing for a church, for instance, there is a recognised comprehensive language of religious symbols which one may draw upon. Most religious symbols are simple, direct shapes; many are purely geometric, and can be combined and related with each other when applied to basic design. (Colour plate 28.) It is worthwhile taking the time to study and discover the symbolism connected with the subject of the commission, in order to communicate clearly and concisely to the viewer. If the symbolic language of a particular subject appears to be limited, it is up to the designer to be imaginative and invent suitable signs. For instance, in a commission for a maternity hospital – the subject being *Creation and Growth* – the study of the shapes of human cells, sperm, and ova produced a series of symbols which were incorporated into the design, conveying the message easily to those who understood that particular language. (Figs. 9–3 and 4.)

Working on a commission for an individual, where the work is to be hung in a private house or an office, constitutes a more personal situation. Many of the considerations discussed above do not affect the designer to the same extent and there is much more scope for expressing one's own ideas.

A commissioned embroidery is generally considered to be a durable work, something which will be seen and enjoyed by many people for a considerable number of years, though this naturally depends on the subject matter and the situation in which it will be displayed. A design for an altar frontal in a cathedral would have a different function and life span from a hanging or panel in a hotel foyer, and this aspect controls not only the design itself, but the materials and methods of working. (Colour plate 25.) A design for a church embroidery should have an almost eternal quality about it (Figs. 9–5 and 6.), unaffected by contemporary design trends which would be effective for a short time, but become extremely dated and therefore unsatisfactory later. This also directs the embroiderer to include only the highest quality materials and threads in a work of this nature – materials which will withstand the effects of light, dust, and handling. The techniques involved should be chosen carefully in order to produce the best possible result, not only for appearance but also for durability. (Fig. 9–7.) The highest level of craftsmanship should be maintained throughout the commission, if the embroiderer is aiming at the aesthetic perfection that comes from the exquisite balance of timeless design, beautiful quality, and excellent portrayal. (Fig. 9–8.)

For commissioned work of a more temporary nature,

Fig. 9–4. *Detail of* Animal, Vegetable and Mineral.

on the other hand, considerations of materials and methods may be regarded from a different viewpoint. In this situation, the emphasis can be on a more up-to-date approach towards the design content, and can incorporate a wider range of materials. More experimental methods of executing the design can be introduced, achieving a totally different impression from that created for Church embroidery.

Each new commission presents a different set of considerations and problems, which act as a challenge to the imagination, knowledge, and ingenuity of the embroiderer. Ideally, the result is a work which is satisfying to its creator and acceptable to its promoter.

Fig. 9–5. *Detail of inset panel for Communion Table (see Colour plate 25). The combination of finely drawn leaves and the use of transparent materials over gold and other colours creates a sensitive background for the simple treatment of the flower itself.* (Property of Sherbrooke St Gilbert's Church, Glasgow.) Mary Pilpak.

Fig. 9–6. Resurrection. *Small panel of brightly coloured embroidery on a three-dimensional cross. The embroidery extends on to the white background.* Jan Machesney.

Fig. 9–7. *Detail of* Passion-Flower Pulpit Fall *(see Colour plate 27)*.
*The free drawing of laid gold threads forming the 'crown of thorns'*
*contrasts with the formality of the solid gold circle and the raised cross*.
(Property of Colmonell Church, Ayrshire.) Hannah Frew.

Fig. 9–8. Silver Cross. *Three-dimensional silver cross on a background of white Thailand silk, built up in stages towards the centre. Various methods of construction are employed, including the use of silver purl, Japanese silver, beads, sequins, and silver kid.* (Photograph by Harry Blake, Strathaven.) Hannah Frew.

# Bibliography

COLBY, A. *Patchwork*, B. T. Batsford Limited, London (1958)

COLBY, A. *Quilting*, B. T. Batsford Limited, London (1972)

COATS, J. and P. *100 Embroidery Stitches*

CRITCHLOW, K. *Order in Space*, Thames and Hudson, London (1969)

FITZRANDOLPH, M. *Traditional Quilting*, B. T. Batsford Limited, London (1954)

GREGORY, R. L. *The Intelligent Eye*, Weidenfeld and Nicolson, London (1970)

HICKETHIER, A. *Colour Matching and Mixing*, B. T. Batsford Limited, London (1970)

HUGHES, T. *English Domestic Needlework*, Lutterworth Press, London (1961)

ITTEN, J. *The Art of Color*, Van Nostrand Reinhold, New York (1962)

SNOOK, B. *English Historical Embroidery*, B. T. Batsford Limited, London (1960)

SNOOK, B. *Embroidery Stitches*, B. T. Batsford Limited, London (1963)

SYMONDS AND PREECE *Needlework Through the Ages*, Hodder and Stoughton Limited, London (1928)

THOMAS, M. *Dictionary of Embroidery Stitches*, Hodder and Stoughton Limited, London (1934)

THOMAS, R. K. *Three-Dimensional Design. A Cellular Approach*, Van Nostrand Reinhold, New York (1970)

VICTORIA AND ALBERT MUSEUM *Guide to English Embroidery* (1970)

WHYTE, K. *Design in Embroidery*, B. T. Batsford Limited, London (1969)

# Suppliers

## UNITED STATES

### GENERAL EQUIPMENT
Boutique Margot, 26 West 54th St., New York, N.Y.
American Crewel Studio, Box 553, Westfield, N.J. 07091
American Thread Corporation, 90 Park Avenue, New York, N.Y.
Bucky King Embroideries Unlimited, 121 South Drive, Pittsburgh,
    Penn. 15238
The Needle's Point Studio, 1626 Macon St., McLean, Va. 22101

### THREADS AND YARNS
*Crewel and tapestry wools*
Appleton Bros., West Main Rd., Little Compton, Rhode Island 02837
American Crewel Studio, Box 553, Westfield, N.J. 07091
Boutique Margot, 26 West 54th St., New York, N.Y.
*Lily line thread*
Lily Mills Co., Shelby, N. Carolina 28150
*General machine and hand embroidery threads, macramé cord etc.*
Robin and Russ Handweavers, 533 North Adams St., McMinnville,
    Oregon 97128
Boutique Margot, 26 West 54th St., New York, N.Y.
American Thread Corporation, 90 Park Avenue, New York, N.Y.
Bucky King Embroideries Unlimited, 121 South Drive, Pittsburgh,
    Penn. 15238
The Needle's Point Studio, 1626 Macon St., McLean, Va. 22101
Yarn Bazaar, Yarncrafts Ltd., 3146 M. St., N.W. Washington D.C.
*Scrap leather*
Bill Levine Leather Corp., 17 Cleveland Place, New York, N.Y. 10012
Tandy Leather Co. Inc., P.O. Box 791, Fort Worth, Texas 76101
    (also 140 retail outlets throughout the U.S.)
MacLeather Co., 424 Broome St., New York, N.Y.
Aerolyn Fabrics Inc., 380 Broadway, New York, N.Y.
*Gold and silver kid*
Aerolyn Fabrics Inc., 380 Broadway, New York, N.Y.

### FABRICS
Fe-Ro Fabrics, 147 West 57th St., New York, N.Y.
*Imported natural fibres*
Jerry Brown, 85 Hester St., New York, N.Y.
*Plastic*
Almac Plastics, 47-42 37th St., Long Island City, N.Y. 11101
Port Plastics, 180 Constitution Drive, Menlo Park, Calif. 94025
Plasticrafts, 2800 North Speer, Denver, Colorado 80211

### DECORATIONS
*Beads, pearls, glass, shells etc.*
Sidney Coe Inc., 65 West 37th St., New York, N.Y.
Arareity, 1021 R St., Sacramento, California
Bethlehem Imports, 5231 Cushman Place, San Diego, Calif. 92110

## GREAT BRITAIN

### GENERAL EQUIPMENT
The Needlewoman, 146 Regent St., London W.1
Harrods Ltd., Knightsbridge, London S.W.1
John Lewis, Oxford St., London W.1
Mace & Nairn, 89 Crane St., Salisbury, Wilts.
MacCulloch & Wallis Ltd., 25-26 Dering St., London W.1
Christine Riley, 58 Barclay St., Stonehaven, Kincardineshire
The Hobby Horse, 52 Montgomery St., Eaglesham, Renfrewshire

### THREADS AND YARNS
*Crewel and tapestry wools*
Appleton Bros., Church St., Chiswick, London W.4
*D.M.C. threads*
C & F Handicraft Suppliers, 246 Stag Lane, Kingsbury,
    London N.W.9
*Machine embroidery threads*
MacCulloch & Wallis Ltd., 25-26 Dering St., London W.1
C & F Handicraft Suppliers, 246 Stag Lane, Kingsbury,
    London N.W.9
The Needlewoman, 146 Regent St., London W.1.
*Fancy cottons and wools*
T. M. Hunter, Sutherland Mills, Brora, Scotland
Craftsman's Mark Ltd., Trefnant, Denbigh, N. Wales, LL16 5UD
J. Hyslop Bathgate & Co., Victoria Works, Galashiels, Scotland
*Metal thread embroidery suppliers*
Mace & Nairn, 89 Crane St., Salisbury, Wilts.
Louis Grosse Ltd., 36 Manchester St., London W.1
The Royal School of Needlework, 25 Princes Gate, London S.W.7
Benton & Johnston, Stephen Simpson, 26 Marshalsea Rd.,
    London S.E.1

### FABRICS
John Lewis, Oxford St., London W.1
Harrods Ltd., Knightsbridge, London S.W.1
Liberty & Co., Regent St., London W.1
*Furnishing fabrics*
Sanderson & Co., 56 Berners St., London W.1
Sekers Fabrics Ltd., 190 Sloane St., London S.W.1
Tibor Ltd., Clifford Mill, Stratford-on-Avon, Warwicks.
*Specialist suppliers*
The Needlewoman, 146 Regent St., London W.1
Mrs Mary Allen, Turnditch, Derbyshire
The Royal School of Needlework, 25 Princes Gate, London S.W.7
Mace & Nairn, 89 Crane St., Salisbury, Wilts.
MacCulloch & Wallis, 25-26 Dering St., London W.1
Christine Riley, 58 Barclay St., Stonehaven, Kincardineshire
The Hobby Horse, 52 Montgomery St., Eaglesham, Renfrewshire
*Linen scrim*
Nottingham Handicraft Co., Milton Rd., West Bridford, Nottingham
Lockhart & Sons Ltd., Linktown Works, Kirkcaldy, KY1 1QH
Dicksons & Co. Ltd., Dungannon, Co. Tyrone, N. Ireland
*Handwoven silks*
Liberty & Co., Regent St., London W.1
*Wadding, interlinings and stiffenings*
MacCulloch & Wallis, 25-26 Dering St., London W.1
Vilene Information, Greetland, Halifax, HX4 8NJ
*Leather*
The Light Leather Co., 16 Soho Square, London W.1
R. & A. Kohnstamm Ltd., Randack Tannery, Croydon Rd.,
    Beckenham, Kent
Messrs Pittard, Sherbrook Rd., Yeovil, Somerset (remnants)
*Gold and silver kid (whole skins only)*
Mace & Nairn, 89 Crane St., Salisbury, Wilts.
The Light Leather Co., 16 Soho Square, London W.1
*Plastic*
John Lewis (Furnishing Dept.), Oxford St., London W.1

### DECORATIONS
*Jewels, beads, sequins and trimmings*
Ells & Farrier, 5 Princes Street, London W.1
Bourne & Hollingsworth Ltd., Oxford St., London W.1
Rubans de Paris, 39a Maddox St., London W.1
*Shisha glass*
Maharani Ltd., 10 Quadrant Arcade, 80-82 Regent St., London W.1

# Index